May you always
remember your ed
is in Christ !!!.
Dr. Jackie Dorsaney
4/23/16

IT: Identity Trespass

Myth of Self Esteem and
Truth of God Esteem

Jacqueline DeLaney

authorHOUSE®

AuthorHouse™
1663 Liberty Drive
Bloomington, IN 47403
www.authorhouse.com
Phone: 1 (800) 839-8640

Published by AuthorHouse   01/28/2016

ISBN: 978-1-5049-7573-5 (sc)
ISBN: 978-1-5049-7572-8 (e)

Dedicated to my children, grandchildren, and church family

TABLE OF CONTENTS

A proud mind is high conceit self-esteem, and carnal aspiring;
A humble mind is high indeed in God esteem and in holy aspiring.
Martin Luther

PREFACE

Every human being has an innate call to be truly known as significant, and loved by others. God has created, and set this longing within us to be known, for who we are. Knowing you is to know that your identity is in Jesus Christ, because you were created in God's image. An individual's lack of this knowledge can result in a socio-psychological "identity crisis" and "role confusion" as characterized by social psychologist, Erik Erikson. To know your identity, is to know whose you are, and how you came to be you. Therefore, much of our emotional pain, turmoil, and dysfunctions in our personal lives are predicated on not knowing our true identity. Essentially, we make an effort to behave according to our self-concept and self-esteem, which are based on our versions of reactions we have received from others. Consequently, self-esteem points toward the distinction between one's perceived self-concept and with one's ideal self.

Our sense of worth is initially, tremendously impacted during our early years; because we develop a vision of ourselves through the expressions we received by the significant people during those early years. Loving affirmations promote good self-identity, and being rejected can be the basis for a negative self-image later in life. Due to such unprocessed emotionally trauma from our early years, many of us experience core longings deficits. Also, these unprocessed emotional wounds impact our relationships with God, self, and others. Consequently, we need the aid of a structure that promotes the truth of God-esteem, and to position us for emotional healing that positively impact our identity in Christ. This book presents elements of a Spiritual formational approach, which incorporates the knowledge of core longings, self-fulfilling behaviors, and emotional wounds into a personal healing structure that impacts Christian identity.

The outgrowth of this book is predicated on my Doctor of Ministry's dissertation project. The focus of the project was to impact Christian identity among a small group of eight participants at St. James Christian Center, Columbus, Ohio through participating in a Pathways curriculum. The intent for this group was to impact the participants' understanding of how core longings, the perception of God, self and others impact their Christian identity. According to the Pathways curriculum, core longings are defined as follows:

> What we name as core longings, love, purpose, understanding, security, belonging, and significance were initially experienced by Adam and Eve as blessings—*the blessings belonging to God*. They were the very basis of their identity and their sense of connectedness and purpose. (Thomas and Frank 2009, 3)

The Pathways curriculum's structure includes a teaching component, an experiential component, and a spiritual component. Each group session was held weekly for two hours over a period of eight weeks. The content of the curriculum initially conveyed to the participants, God's unconditional love and pathway to experiencing God's blessings or core longings. The participants received knowledge that after the fall, humankind's consciousness of God was distorted, resulting in them experiencing "core longing deficits". Conversely, the participants recognized how God designed a plan of restoration in Jesus Christ through the power of the Holy Spirit for humankind. The participants learned how their emotional wounds and dysfunctional behaviors negatively impact their relationships with God, self and others. They also were taught how to incorporate their core longings, self-fulfilling behaviors, and emotional wounds into a personal healing structure that impacts their Christian identity.

This book examined the relationship of core longings to Christian identity, in view of the following biblical themes: Humanity as created in the image of God; the fall; and restoration of Christian identity rooted in the identity of Jesus Christ. As stated above, an individual's lack of this knowledge can result in a socio-psychological "identity crisis" and "role confusion" as characterized by social psychologist, Erik Erikson in his developmental model identified as "theory of development" (Erikson 1963). Therefore, a correct image of one's identity that is grounded in biblical scripture is crucial in impacting one's Christian identity.

The central thread throughout the bible is God's redemptive plan of love for humankind. Included in this plan of redemption, God has provided a plan for Christian identity through the work of Jesus Christ by the power of the Holy Spirit, which is the central theme of this book.

The biblical foundation in this book discusses the following: (1) Aspects on how God created humankind in His image; (2) The fall of humankind; and (3) God's planned redemption for humankind. The bible reveals how God's Son, Jesus Christ, reconciled humankind back to God, including the provision for a new identity in Him. The bible further expounds on this new identity as being rooted in the identity of Jesus Christ.

Theologically in this book, the foundation concentrates on the magnitude for humankind to have a vivid consciousness, that they are the beloved of God. Also, the theological foundation points out the connection of Christian identity with core longings, or blessings of God.

Constructed in the historical foundation of this book, is how the Church has shaped meaning relative to Christian identity within the historical universal Church, which is rooted in the centrality of Jesus Christ.

Addressing the contemporary foundation in this book, are the views of various contemporary authors pertaining to impacting Christian identity. Taken as a whole, these foundations sustain the general concept of this book.

INTRODUCTION: IDENTITY QUESTION

Who are you? What is your identity? These are questions often answered by people in terms of their occupation, profession or service to others with such responses as the following: "I am a parent." "I am a minister." "I am a teacher." On other occasions, people will produce an identification badge or card to answer the question, who am I? In pondering over these questions and responses, I came across the following:

> Have you ever met a man who is the center of attention wherever he goes? . . Well, that's the way it was two thousand years ago with Jesus Christ . . . . He never wrote a book, commanded an army, held a political office, or owned property. He mostly traveled within a hundred miles of his village . . . . Jesus changed the world for the next 20 centuries . . . that unknown carpenter's son from Nazareth. (Chapman, 2012)

To know your identity is to know who you are, and how you came to be you. More important, knowing you is to know that your identity is in Jesus Christ, because you were created in the image of God.

Much of humankind's emotional pain is predicted on not knowing their identity in Christ, and in whose image they were created. Through

1

the lens of formational counseling and prayer principles, developed by Dr. Terry Wardle (professor, theologian, author, and founder of Healing Care Ministries), this book was designed with the expressed purpose of impacting Christian identity in others. Marcus Borg, author and theologian, points out that fundamental to one's identity and self-worth is their Christian identity formation. Furthermore, Borg emphasizes that Christian identity formation is the most fundamental meaning of the Christian Gospel. In fact, he goes on to explain his assumption in an uncomplicated recognizable way as follows: "You are created by God; You are a child of God; You are beloved by God; and You are accepted by God" (Borg 2003, 191). Therefore, a deficient knowledge of our true identity in Christ will result in much emotional turmoil and dysfunctions in our personal lives. Several years ago, I attended an event and heard Maya Angelou, (1928-2014) author and poet, articulate that, "When we know better, we will do better". Therefore, our identity in Christ is impacted with knowledge of who we are in Christ.

As part of my role as a pastoral care counselor at my church, I met with a new member, who was in the process of divorcing her second husband. She expressed feelings of shame and bewilderment to be in another situation of a failed marriage. It is important to note, that both of her previous husbands are church pastors. However, there are no children from either marriage. She informed me that, not only, is she a third generation Christian, but has been an active and faithful participant in church most of her life. Nonetheless, she expressed being very confused about her blindness to similar dysfunctional personality traits in her second husband that she experienced with her first husband. She also wonders why she does not feel good enough about herself, and often compares herself with others.

I also learned that her parents divorced when she was in elementary school. What's more, throughout childhood, she experienced many disappointments with her father's erratic weekend visitations. Therefore, she often created a rationale for his absenteeism, to avoid any negative opinions from others. Yet, she is grateful to her mother and maternal grandmother for their nurture, provisions, and religious affiliation with her church denomination.

To my chagrin, this person withdrew her membership from our church before our second meeting. Approximately three weeks after our meeting, her divorce became final from her second husband, and that same week she relocated to another city. However, within a few days of her relocation, she married again for the third time. Her new husband also is a pastor of a church.

The above story can be well defined within the framework of Dr. Terry Wardle's "Structures of Healing Model". The *Healing Care Groups Curriculum: Leader's Guide* states the *life situation* relates to *dysfunctional behavior*. This behavior then transmits to *emotional upheaval* that relates to *lies and distortions* that shape emotional wounds (Wardle 2001, 4-6). As a result, out of this structure, many Christians experience a false personal identity. This faulty identity is often rooted in the negative messages received from those significant people in the early years of life. Therefore, Christians are oblivious to their Christian identity. Neil Anderson points out the following:

> . . . your hope for growth, meaning and fulfillment as a Christian is based on understanding who you are— specifically, your identity in Christ as a child of God. Your understanding of who God is and who you are in relationship to Him is the critical foundation for your belief system and your behavior patterns as a Christian. (Anderson 2000, 24)

Our Christian identity must be based on the truth of our relationship with our Heavenly Father.

Unfortunately, there are many Christians who characterize themselves based on perverse early life messages received from other emotionally wounded people. The recipients of such messages experience an internal "personal identity crisis". As a result, when we lack knowledge of our identity in Christ, our belief system is distorted, and these distorted beliefs can contribute to our identity crisis. However, in our understanding the fundamentals of core longings, we will impact our Christian identity. According to Thomas and Frank, these blessings come from God, and are the basis of our identity, sense of our connectedness and purpose (Thomas and Frank 2009, 3).

My personal experience in formational prayer and counseling at Ashland Theological Seminary has enlightened me to the significance on the subject of impacting Christian identity in others. Therefore, I am extremely motivated to share the information about this transformational experience with others. Dr. Terry Wardle ignited this motivation in me during my time on the campus of Ashland Theological Seminary in the Doctor of Ministry program.

I remember very vividly the tears rolling down my face as Dr. Wardle responded to a statement I made in class. It was pertaining to me being overly concerned and critical about my performance in a situation outside of class. Dr. Wardle turned and moved directly in front of me, as he looked directly at me, he said, "Jackie, you are beloved, and you are chosen, and you are empowered by God. There is nothing you can do to make Him love you anymore, and there is nothing you can do to make Him love you any less." As I heard those words from Dr. Wardle, I experienced the very presence of the Holy Spirit. It seemed to me, at that moment; Jesus was speaking directly to me. It was a defining moment for me. It was also the beginning of my emotional healing journey toward "knowing and feeling" that my "self" has significance rooted in my identity in Christ. I want others to experience this kind of "eye-opener" within their beings.

Since the church, as a component of spiritual formation, is to impact believers' Christian identity, it is crucial that it become more vigilant in this transformational process. This formational process works best in a "small group forum" over a certain period of time spent together outside of the "Sunday Morning" worship experience. This process has the ability to become, by and large, a ministry within the church that assists the Pastor in the area of member discipleship, which is necessary throughout one's earthly journey.

Such a ministry, in the church, creates a pathway for us to witness the power of God in working through our emotional weaknesses. We can then, more adamantly, identify with the Apostle Paul: "and it is no longer I who live, but it is Christ who lives in me. And the life I now live in the flesh I live by faith in the Son of God, who loved me and gave himself for me" (Gal. 2:20). All Scripture references in this book are from the NRSV translation unless otherwise noted.

CHAPTER TWO:
CONTEMPORARY FOUNDATION
OF IDENTITY

I embark upon this chapter with a comment that I recently heard on the radio from Oprah Winfrey (television host and current owner of the OWN television network). She said:

> Every human being is looking for one thing, and that is to be validated, to be seen and to be heard . . . at the end of almost every interview in one form or another, somebody would always lean in and say, 'was that okay?' After interviewing numerous guests on my program for twenty-five seasons, I started to see that pattern. And what I realized is that everybody is looking for the same thing. No matter if it is politicians, senators, presidents, Beyonce in all of her Beyonce-ness. We are all looking to know did you see me, did you hear me, and did what I say mean anything to you. So just saying hello is a way of validating even a stranger. (February, 2015)

The above words seem to tell us that as humans, we need to know that we matter to others. According to Dr. Wardle, author and professor at Ashland Seminary, "Everyone wants to know that they matter and have a special place at the table of life" (Wardle 2004, 27). We have an innate call to be truly known as significant and loved by others. God has created and set this longing within us to be loved and known for who we are. What is more, our true identity is not to be grounded in what people think of us, but in how God views and values us (Shaw 2013, x). Humankind has been magnificently made by God, and given by Him relational blessings that are manifested as core longings.

Due to our unprocessed emotionally trauma from our early years, many us experience core longings deficits. Therefore, we need the aid of a structure to position us for healing that will positively impact our identity in Christ. Formational counseling provides a model that provides the needed structure for emotional healing in broken people. "Formational counseling is a ministry of Christian care-giving that integrates pastoral care, spiritual direction, and spirit-directed counseling with a view to bringing hope, healing, and spiritual well-being to broken people" (Wardle, 2003).

Core Longings

Humankind was created by God to experience special relational blessings defined by Dr. Anne Halley as core longings. God made humans to: "feel, desire and experience love, security, understanding, purpose, significance and belonging" (Halley 2009, 10). Therefore, we were created to experience complete love, security, to be fully understood, to know our purpose, to feel significant, and to know that we belong to our Creator. As recorded in Genesis (Gen. 1:31), the first book of the Bible, before the fall, Adam and Eve experienced these unconditional blessings from God, and enjoyed a harmonious relationship with Him. However, the sin of Adam and Eve resulted in their relational brokenness with God. This sin distorted their thinking, in that; they were alone without any direction to figure out how to meet their own core longings. Shaw also finds that this distorted thinking and broken relationship with God led to the beginning of humankind's modification of self-identity (Shaw 2013, xiv). Therefore, the quest to answer the question of identity continues in humankind.

"Who are you?" is a question Neil Anderson asks regarding humankind's identity. He alleges that this question may appear to be a simple inquiry requiring a simple answer. Yet it can be a very difficult question for many people to answer (Anderson 2000, 23). The answer is not simple, because of humans' ambiguous search in seeking significance in their identity. Eric Geiger agrees that, "Everyone searches for a clear identity. We long to possess a strong sense of who we are. And we crave to be known for something" (Geiger 2008, 7). We have a need to unequivocally be known and understood by others, which produces significance in our identity.

When we are unaware of our identity, we will look for meaning in things, relationships, money, and in any other way that presents itself to us. "People everywhere are wearing themselves out trying to find a way to stand out from the crowd and be recognized as a unique and a special human being" (Wardle 2004, 25). We yearn to experience the consciousness of significance within ourselves. Since significance is synonymous with meaning, it is connected to human identity (Shaw 2013, xv). As Wardle and Shaw both point out, God has created each of us with the blessing of significance.

Early Life Attachment Formation

Kirwan finds our significance, or sense of self worth, develops from a vision of ourselves through the expressions we have received by the significant people in our early years of life. Loving affirmations throughout our lives promote good self-identity and self-image. Being rejected by significant others in our early formative years can be the basis for a negative self-image later in life (Kirwan 1984, 74). Consequently, much of our emotional development is a result of our attachments and relationships with our parents or primary caregivers during our formative years.

Along these lines, Siegel and Hartzell explain how these early attachments affect our primary foundation for our emotional interactions with others. Poor attachments in these early years can even have a negative impact on early brain growth. Unmet attachment needs due to one's parent's behavior can cause disorientation, which may develop into disorganized attachments to others. Nevertheless, our emotional problems are by no means beyond repair and healing. It is important to note that since we are social people, it is always possible to receive healing from our early experiences. One healing method is through the process of sharing our narratives. As we network and share with others, we can heal our past wounds (Siegel and Hartizell 2003, 132). Thus, emotional and spiritual growth is enhanced through relational attachment with others.

Anne Halley writes that in the absence of healthy attachments to improve our developmental process of emotional and spiritual growth, we remain unaware of our Christian identity (Halley2009, 24). This lack of awareness also prevents us from connecting to our core longings, which are blessings from God. However, humans were formed by God to mature and be in fellowship with Him as they experience His nurturing presence. This is physically possible, because God devised humankind's neurological brain structure (Halley 2009, 24). Our physical brains are designed to provide us the ability to be in relationship with God.

The significance of early brain development in relation to attachment theory is included in the formational inner healing model. According to this model, we observe an integration of the following three important notions: "(1) The current research on brain, trauma, and childhood development; (2) Spiritual development and direction; and (3) Christian empathic response" (Halley 2009, 16). We as humans have been created to be in relationship with God and other social beings. Daniel Siegel, founder of Interpersonal Neurobiology, concludes that we exist within the interactions of people in families, communities, including the world at large, and they have impacted the formation our social brains. Cozolino, consequently, finds the progression of our culture continu continually impacts how we learn to understand ourselves, and to commune with others (Cozolino 2010, x). Therefore, it is imperative to understand that the humankind has a physical brain, which has a need for social attachment with other human beings.

Again Siegel and Hartzell see (along with Halley) the complexity of understanding the fundamental nature of what it means to be human has been discussed for centuries. Included in these discussions are personality developmental theories, which insist God created humans with knowledge (obtained prenatally) about their emotional being (Halley 2009, 16). Furthermore, it has been discovered that emotional attachment and bonding occurs while the baby is in its mother's womb. We know also that our consciousness (or the soul), the intellect (or the mind) perform as one unit in the physical brain. Neuroscience studies have found that these mental processes are the result of neuron activity firing within the brain (Siegel and Hartzell 2003, 31). The brain is a complicated part of humankind according to the following:

> The human psyche, defined as the soul, the intellect, and the mind, is a functioning entity that is believed to be a process that emerges from the activity of the brain. The brain, an integrated system of the body itself, has been explored in the exploding new findings of neuroscience. (Siegel and Hartzell 2003, 31)

The consciousness of humans materializes from the movement of neurons that occur inside the brain.

Halley points out that a neuron is a vital cell in the tissues of the human brain. Neurons are environmentally sensitive, and transmit this sensitive information to other neurons, which signal the body to respond accordingly. In as much as a large part of the brain's wiring is genetic that provides axons to travel the right pathways; this process is dependent on sensory awareness acquired during our early years of life. Neurons connect to each other and provide synapses to stimulate the nerves. Acting as the neuron's antennae are dendrites that appear like tree branches. Dendrites are coated with thousands of synapses as receptors to sense the neurotransmitters, which are chemically signaled. These signals arrive from electrical impulses, and are stored in the axon with the ability to repeatedly convert into electrical information. This process provides the brain's mechanism for computational abilities (Halley 2002, 18). God has designed an intricate physiology referred to as the brain for humankind to receive information and know its awareness as a being.

Cozolino's discussion on early childhood research demonstrates that early nurturance has a significant impact on the social brain. Therefore, if we experience early relationships that are abusive and inappropriate, our brain becomes accustomed to the veracity of such negative circumstances. There is neural research that concludes within relationally close connections, abusive experiences can remain over a lifespan. When a child's social brain has been shaped in such a context, it impacts learning, memory and attachment in relationships (Cozolino 2010, 227). This author also points out the following:

> When our early relationships are frightening, abusive, or nonexistent, our brains dutifully adapt to the realities of our unfortunate situations. However, there is reason to believe that these circuits retain experience-dependent plasticity throughout life, especially in close relationships. (Cozolino 2010, 227)

Research in neuroscience has increased our knowledge of child development and the area in theory of attachment.

Attachment theory demonstrates parent/child interactions will impact children's future developmental pathways, including their mental processes (Siegel, Hartzell 2003, 31). These interactional ways of communication models that children experience in their early years with parents or caregivers provide influential evidence on the child's maturity. Allan Schore adds that, "these early socio-emotional events are imprinted into the biological structures that are maturing during the early brain growth spurt, and therefore have long enduring effects" (Schore 2002, 249). Environmental factors have an enormous impact on the brain during rapid brain development.

The brain's mental processes are affected by the relationships people form. This juncture of scientific knowledge with interpersonal neurobiology offers a structure to comprehend everyday occurrences of parent and child interactions. The move toward interpersonal neurobiology is supported by the following theories: (1) the mental process is a flow of energy and information; (2) this flow materializes in the matter of neuron-physiological processes and interpersonal relationships; and (3) the mind matures genetically and according to how the brain responds to continuing experiences (Seigel and Hartzell 2003, 32). The way we give meaning to the stream of knowledge that goes through our minds, will determine our perception of that knowledge.

Seigel and Hartzell enhances our understanding of the brain in the argument that humankind is born with an undeveloped brain, and is dependent upon others for its vital concerns; when compared with many other species. Due to the immaturity of a newborn's brain, environmental experiences have a great position in the development of its brain linkages. Consequently, the baby's experiences will impact its brain formation and facilitate the baby's perceptions of those experiences (Seigel and Hartzell 2003, 33). A healthy environment is paramount for optimal brain development in infants.

Nevertheless, Bowlby takes the idea that a baby's capability to build upon actions that cause its mother or caretaker to react is established at birth. For example, the baby swiftly gains knowledge that crying will draw attention. As a result, the baby learns to smile, and realizes that it is another tool to get attention. As the baby grows, it learns more behaviors for attention. Then the goal of the child becomes to keep its mother or caretaker close for a feeling of security. John Bowlby (1907-1990), a psychoanalyst in the theory of attachment, as discussed by Leick and Davidsen-Nielsen, considers that the magnitude for close attachment of the baby to one or more persons is proportionally known, as the same importance, as it is for the baby's food (Leick and Davidsen-Nielsen 1991, 8). Healthy brain development is extremely dependent on early attachment of babies to their mothers or significant caretakers.

Halley further explains, attachment is defined as "an emotional and neurobiological bond that occurs between the mother and the child" (Halley 2009, 21). It is an unprompted affect ant transaction between the child and its mother or caretaker. Some theorists argue that cognitive development propels the altering in the attachment system from behavior to emotional representations. Yet, the theme proposed in this book follows Viviane Green, that attachment is important in cognitive development. The ability for psychologically sharing and interpreting each other's experiences is exclusively human. Human attachment also provides a chief discerning benefit for the development of social intelligence. Attachment is a framework that permits an infant to develop its own sensitivity. Also, attachment in humans provides a capacity for sensitivity to a second order of symbolic representation, such as desires and beliefs (Green 2003, 115).

The representational system of the developmental process has its origins in the baby's internalization of the mother's mirror response to its anguish. The empathic state of the mother presents emotional feedback to the baby, which is a secondary representation of its emotional status (Green 2003, 115). At this point, the baby does not have the ability to separate its mother's experience from its own self's experience. Nonetheless, Halley adds that it is through this process the foundation of attachment and the regulation of one's own emotions take place. For that reason, during the child's emotional crisis, a mother connecting at an empathic level facilitates the child's ability to return to a serene state (Halley 2009, 22). The mother provides the child a safe place to repair emotionally, and establish a state of trust and security within itself.

The Developing Self

Historically, several psychologists have put forward various theories on the development of the human self. Among these psychologists are the following: Sigmund Freud (1856-1939) speaks of the fulfillment of drives; Erich Fromm (1900-1980) theorizes about the need for self-love; Carl Rogers (1902-1987) is connected with unconditional positive regard; Erik Erikson (1902-1994) structures the psychosocial stages of life development; John Bowlby (1907-1990) is known for the importance early experience with attachment caretakers; Abraham Maslow (1908-1970) refers to a hierarchy of needs concept; and Heinz Kohut (1913-1981) theorizes on the psychology of the self. These are just a few known psychological theorists. While we continue to learn from these individuals, many of their theories are based in the belief that the soul is satisfied through self-love only. However, Mintle says we know that the self is developed in the milieu of others because we are relational beings (Mintle 2002, 4-5). These theorists provide a structure and framework to better comprehend the progression of human development pertaining to the self. Therefore, we understand that we form our self-identities through our attachments to others and our interactions and actions within the community.

Rivera concludes that constructing self-identity is initiated at birth, shaped by family, community and faith (Rivera 2014). In order to discuss self-identity, it is necessary to discuss the make-up of the human self. A self is a consistent way of being, and experiencing one's environment. Dawes agrees, and says the self matures to an awareness of its being that is recognizable to one's self (Dawes 2010). The optimal self has a conscious awareness of its thoughts and behaviors within its environment. As the self develops and becomes more aware of its distinctiveness, it acquires a self-concept based on its reflection and sentiments about itself. Self-concept may be defined as self-esteem or self-worth, which can result in the self maturing to understand its exclusive human identity within its community.

Self-Concept and Self-Esteem

An important input for this discussion on the developing self is a description of the correlation between self-concept and self-esteem. While the meaning of these two concepts can be closely aligned, for this book, each one will be discussed separately. One's self-concept is a general inspection of how one perceives oneself. Plummer believes this perception comprises one's appearance, ability, temperament, attitudes and beliefs, which are weighted toward one's version of reactions one has received from others. Essentially, we make an effort to behave according to our self-concept. Therefore, if we ascertain new information about ourselves, we will dismiss it, if we perceive it to be irrelevant to our belief system. However, if the information compares to be the same as our self-concept (even if not supported by truth), we will most likely agree with it (Plummer 2005, 14). Self-concept is how people scrutinize themselves as a whole, which includes all aspects of their selves.

A healthy self-esteem can also be considered as possessing a positive self-regard of one's competence, and feeling lovable with the approval of others. Despite the fact that self-esteem entails appraisal of the self-concept, it is frequently dissimilar to one's true abilities. However, individuals have diverse levels of self-esteem in different contexts. Therefore, the degree of self-esteem in specific life areas is based on the rank of importance placed on each area by the individual. Consequently, self-esteem points toward the distinction between one's perceived self-concept and with one's ideal self. Subsequently, if an individual sees him/herself close to his or her ideal self, the individual is considered to have a healthy self-esteem. The ideal self does not necessarily mean the perfect self. However, an individual with a low self-esteem, might well construct idealistic concepts of a desired self, or create concepts of how the self should be constructed (Plummer 2005, 14).

The overall positive early childhood experiences promote one to internalize feelings of self-worth, thereby with less reliance on others for approval. Plummer suggests the following:

> As young children we rely heavily on external means to confirm our self-worth and competence. We look to the significant people in our lives (parents, grandparents, teachers, etc.) . . . An infant coming into the world has no past, no experience in handling himself, no scale on which to judge his own worth. (Plummer 2005, 14)

Our self-concept is developed over time, which stems from how we process others' reactions toward us. We then designate a value on ourselves, which is labeled as "self-esteem.

The Myth of Self-Esteem

Many people, including educators and mental health professionals, are convinced self-esteem is optimal for our emotional well-being. However, Albert Ellis, a renowned clinical psychologist, contended self-esteem is a myth. Ellis was famous for developing a form of psychotherapy called "rational emotive behavior therapy." He suggested self-esteem to be the utmost disorder introduced to humans. According to Ellis, self-esteem endorses individuals applauding themselves when approved by others, and degrading themselves upon receiving disapproval from others. Therefore, Ellis strongly suggested we need self-acceptance rather than self-esteem. He called for people to make the choice to be the master of their life's outcome. He further expounded the following:

> I accept myself, my existence, my being with my fallibility. Too bad about it. But I'm still okay. To define myself

as non-okay—worthless—is silly and will make me more fallible. I'm okay because I think I am. Or, more accurately, I am a person who has many good and many bad traits. (Ellis 2005, 13)

Ellis theorized that an individual's mere existence means in and of itself, worth the right to exist and enjoy the benefits of life. Consequently, all people can be observed as good, because they exist. Ellis's theory seems to project that an individual's worth includes the possession of competency to arrive at good achievements (Ellis 2005, 13).

Negative Self-Image

In contrast, Mintle illustrates that a negative self-image is the negative view held by an individual of his or her own self. Not only is this negative view a cognitive representation within the mind of the individual, but includes the negative way in which the individual talks about their self. Negative self-image comes, in part, from negative responses a person has received from others. With the internalization of the negative responses, the individual eventually acquires this negative information as his or her own concept. This internal dialogue enmeshes as automatic thoughts within the mentality of the individual. As a result, the individual brings these thoughts to a place of feeling inadequate. This distortion in the individual's self evaluation is due to a cloudy vision of the self. In order to correct any distortions, the Holy Spirit and the Word of God is needed to provide the individual with truth and clarity about feelings of inadequate attributes (Mintle 2002, 3-4). In correcting this distorted thinking, it is not to dispense upon us disheartening feelings, but to make use of truthful information. This truth is necessary for Christians in guiding them toward full knowledge of their identity in Christ.

Heinz Kohut's Model of Self Development

Heinz Kohut is noted for developing the theory of self psychology in an endeavor to discover the origin of mental problems through identifying childhood problems. His theory includes the concept that children are sensitive to parental interactions. For emotional and psychological maturity, including optimal brain growth, children need to receive certain habitual approval reactions from their parents (Logan 2015). Kohut's theory primarily substantiates that our sense of self is developed through our interpersonal relationships.

Kohut depicted the self as the core of an individual's psychological make-up. This core consists of the individual's mental capacities, attitudes toward oneself and one's environment. The self is a launching mechanism of one's personality. According to Kohut, a unified healthy self culminates in a sense of personal identity. This identity includes value and meaning, which encourages the full realization of one's abilities. Self development occurs along the following three axes: (1) the grandiosity axis, referring to one's ability to maintain emotional stability; (2) the idealization axis, the ability of a person to maintain a constant system of setting goals; and (3) the alter ego—connectedness axis, or one's ability to converse feelings to others, form personal relationships, and belong to the larger community (Banai, Mikulincer and Shaver 2005). Based on Kohut's theory, the healthy self is a structurally solid product of one's normal development along the above mentioned three axes.

Erik Erikson's Developmental Model

Erik Erikson (1902-1994), a social psychologist, authored the concept of developmental personality theory of nine life-span stages consisting of biological, cultural, and psychosocial factors assimilated within the ego or personality. His theory asserts there is a psychosocial crisis that needs to be resolved at each developmental stage. Erikson influences our understanding of his developmental model, in that; positive and negative factors at each stage are incorporated into the individual's identity. However, a full progression within each stage must take place before the person can successfully move forward to the next stage. With the resolution of each stage's crisis, the person's sense of self and identity are improved. According to Erikson, a new psychological virtue or strength is gained at the conclusion of each stage. Connected to the basic societal stress, is the attending crisis contained in the process of each successive developmental stage (Austrian 2002, 46). Therefore, as the person's life cycle progresses successfully, the person's identity becomes more pronounced.

Birth to eighteen months of age in Erikson's theory, marks the stage of acquiring a sense of trust versus a sense of mistrust. The optimal environment for the baby is when the caretaker meets the baby's needs, which develops its basic trust. Acquiring a sense of autonomy versus a sense of shame and doubt takes place from eighteen months to four years old. At this stage, the child gains more self-control with adult support. Four to six years old, the child gains a sense of initiative versus a sense of guilt. While in this stage, the child sees itself as a person, but the child has the need to maintain identity through identification with its significant adult figure. According to Erikson, the initiation of personality development is connected to the following three social needs: social attention; competence necessary for the environment; and structure in social affairs. Also, Erikson noted that as individuals become stressed later in life, each stage may need to be revisited. Strength is acquired within the individual in the resolution of each crisis (Austrian 2002, 46-50). The process of working through the crisis of each stage makes the individual emotionally stronger.

Erikson's significance of identity formation is well outlined developmentally in what he defines as the adolescence search for the identity stage of adolescence (Johnson, Buboltz, and Seemann 2003). In this stage, Erikson constructs a theory of "identity crisis" and "role confusion" that he classifies as an emotional transition between the early years and adulthood, which requires tenacity to further, describe one's adult identity (Erikson 1963, 261). Metaphorically, many adult Christians can be characterized as being in a spiritual state of "identity crisis" and "role confusion." Eric Ge Geiger asks Christians, "Why are we stuck in spiritual adolescence?" (Geiger 2008, 5). Christians need a spiritual formational model that facilitates formation in their Christian identity in developing their awareness of their relational blessings with God.

CHAPTER THREE:
THE MODEL OF GOD ESTEEM

Devoid of a spiritual formational construct that connects our Christian identity to our core longings, we will search for self-worth in false beliefs. Robert McGee expounds on our search for worth as follows:

> Since the Fall, man has often failed to turn to God for the truth about himself. Instead, he has looked to others to meet his inescapable need for self-worth. I am what others say I am, he has reasoned. I will find my value in their opinions of me. (McGee 2003, 19)

Other people do not have the ability to endow us with the appropriate value for which we most desire. However, God values us so much that He gave His Son as a ransom for us to be reconciled back to Him.

Mintle describes esteem as not being a product of one's accomplishments, or acquired from others. Esteem also is not a feeling that comes from within an individual. Mintle goes on to point out that we, humans, are highly esteemed, because God chose us and created us in His image. Since this fundamental and simplistic truth is antithetical to our sense of individualism, it can be difficult for us to seize and comprehend. Contemporary views promote self-love, self-centeredness and amassing materialistic items. However, as we accept God's Love, we will receive a healthy and strong self-image. Moreover, God wants each individual to incorporate into his or her personal image, the image of Christ (Mintle 2002, 19-20). Scripture points out that Christ's image is that of God. "He is the image of the invisible God . . . ." (Col. 1:15). As we integrate our self-image into the image of Christ, we obtain a healthy self-image. Consequently, God's Love is the solution to all problems of esteem.

Furthermore, cognitively, an individual must re-structure his or her belief system and thought processes to bring about change in his or her view of self. Our acceptance by God is independent of our accomplishments, our appearances, or good deeds. The strategy, therefore, is to have a self-image that is healthy; we must accept God's Love, love God, and permit His Love to be displayed in us. We contain the power to carry out this strategy, because we have been created in God's image. God matures us as we develop an intimate relationship with Him. Without God, we have no capacity to bring ourselves up to God's standard. Nevertheless, God cherishes and recognizes us unconditionally. Since God already esteems us, we do not need to be dependent on others to characterize us as being esteemed (Mintle 2002, 24). Given this enormous beneficial relationship of being in a familiar context with God, we do not need others to define and identify us. God esteems us highly, and provides us with relational blessings. Being aware of these blessings heightens our personal esteem of worth. As a result of our relationship with God, we experience his Love, which is the origin of our esteem.

Authors Ellens and Rollins write that God is characterized in Christianity as definitive in nature, addressing the complete assortment of human needs. From a psychoanalytical perspective, God is referred to as a self-object of human beings. Metaphysically, God is characterized as infinite; which leads to psychoanalytically referring to God as the most grandiose of beings. Finally, they believe it is plausible to view God as being in an empathic relationship with humankind, which is unique to any other self-object (Ellens and Rollins 2004, 259).

From a human standpoint, the comprehension of God is too glorious, that He would be concerned with the commonplace needs of human beings. Yet, on the other hand, we see in Scripture a conversation with God and Moses in the following passage:

> The Lord said to Moses, "I will do the very thing that you have asked; for you have found favor in my sight, and I know you by name." Moses said, "Show me your glory, I pray." And he said, "I will make all my goodness pass before you, and will proclaim before you the name, 'The LORD'. and I will be gracious to whom I will be gracious, and will show mercy on whom I will show mercy. But, "he said, "you cannot see my face; for no one shall see me and live." And the LORD continued, "See, there is a place by me where you shall stand on the rock; and while my glory passed by I will put you in a cleft of the rock, and I will cover you with my hand until I have passes by; then I will take away my hand, and you shall see my back; but my face shall not be seen." (Ex. 33:17-23)

God, in this passage, gives in to Moses's request that He (God) assume the position of the self-object. It is important to note, that God does not assume this position before Moses makes the request. This passage illustrates that the human initiates the transaction, with God exemplifying empathy and taking the position of self-object to Moses. Reflected also in this passage is that Moses takes on the role as God's self-object: According to Ellens and Rollins, Moses request God to "Show me your glory" (Ex. 33:18) and God acquiesces and says, "you have found favor in my sight" (Ex. 33:17). It is apparent that the self and the self-object frequently exchange roles in this passage. God displays His empathic dimension by responding, "I will make all my goodness pass before you" (Ex. 33:19). However, God appends a condition to Moses's request when He says, "You shall see my back, but my face shall not be seen" (Ex. 33:23). God's power transcends humankind's maximum potential to experience such power (Ellens and Rollins 2004, 258). God's provision of empathy to humankind exceeds the magnitude of infinite proportion. Knowing God is always present and concerned with the affairs of humans enormously impacts our God esteem.

Marie Hoffman expounds in her writings that Heinz Kohut's developmental theory supports God esteem. Kohut's theorized that humans have a basic need for an identity in Christ, and to believe in God. According to his theory, the first need is the humans' need of a self-object for idealization. In other words, humans need something to idealize that is perfect. The second human need is for mirroring. In the emotionally broken human being, there is a fundamental image of God that is deep within the human consciousness. The concept of *imago dei* or being created in the very image of God mirrors back to us the precious worth of our humanness. The third need of humans is the need for twin-ship, which is found in the incarnation of Jesus Christ. The embodiment of God, The Son, taking on human form fully knows the human experience. Also, the human need for twin-ship can be experienced within a church community or body of Christian believers (Hoffman 2011, 84). As a member of a church, or community of Christian believers, an individual extends in personal attachment and fellowship with others. This communal experience facilitates a person to internalize their Christian identity as a child of God.

Moreover, optimal Christian communities are biblically grounded, and familiar with the good news recorded in the bible. The information in the bible, through the ministry of the Holy Spirit, has the capacity to equip us to walk worthy in our Christian identity. Terry Wardle explains that "God did not rescue you from the bondage and destructive garbage of the fall, clean you up and then say, 'You're on your own'. No, He stays with you to make sure you have all you need" (Wardle 1998, 201). With this revelation, we can better comprehend that our identities are no longer rooted in our own self-identity. We are fundamentally established in God's Image and Love. Eventually, revelation in our awareness that we are God's creative beings confidently impacts our identity in Christ.

CHAPTER FOUR:
THE FORMATIONAL
COUNSELING MODEL

The knowledge of one's identity according to Mintle, is foundationally indispensable to possessing healthy esteem and a positive self image. Nonetheless, this knowledge must be based on what is truth. The truth is healthy esteem and self image are built on knowledge that humans are created in God's image. Therefore, a mind renewal initiates the development of structuring that knowledge within humans through encompassing a personal identity in Christ. The renewing of the mind comes from understanding that God's Word is necessary in opposing the words downloaded in our minds from other secular sources. These corrections from God's Word will change distorted mindsets to a correct and truthful way of believing who we are in Christ (Mintle 2002, 35). Many of us contain a cognitive data collection of information concerning our identity written in God's Word. Nonetheless, due to our distorted thinking, as a result of traumatic emotional wounding, we may find it difficult to believe an and internalize those biblical facts as truth regarding our identity in Christ.

Formational counseling (introduced earlier in this book) developed by Terry Wardle, professor at Ashland Seminary, is a model of care-giving designed to facilitate transformational change in emotionally wounded individuals through the ministry of the Holy Spirit, toward Christian maturity. This model integrates psychological counseling concepts, spiritual direction, and inner healing prayer through positioning individuals to encounter Jesus Christ's healing presence (Wardle 2001, 12). As an ongoing personal experience for emotionally broken individuals, the Formational Model supports and serves well a process that is structured in formational counseling. This process is one of a growing relationship with God that is conformed to Christ through the ministry work of the Holy Spirit.

Formational counseling model depicted in this book is unique among other spiritual formational models, and attributed in great portion to the passionate work of Dr. Terry Wardle at Ashland Seminary. Therefore, this section will emphasize primarily the work of Dr. Wardle, which has been demonstrated to be valuable in the healing process of emotional wounds within people. He has been on the cutting edge of such practical and biblically based approaches in this area of spiritual formation. This model refers to an intentional process of people encountering Jesus' healing presence for the expressed purpose for healing unprocessed past emotional wounds that negatively impact their identity in Christ.

Often, people will encounter emotional struggles in their pursuit for establishing their identity in Christ. They are primarily hindered due to their untreated past emotional wounds. According to Wardle, "present emotional struggles may be directly related to unprocessed wounding of the past" (Wardle 2007, 61). Therefore, wounded feelings unaddressed at the time of injury will continue to exhibit themselves by way of dysfunctional behaviors in various life situations. Furthermore, Wardle purports, "When people are wounded in life—either by a traumatic event or less stressful experience—it does far more than cause initial pain. It often negatively impacts what they believe about themselves, their world, and God" (Wardle 2007, 72). Consequently, it is likely that untreated emotional wounds in anyone, will distort their beliefs, which ultimately impacts their identity in Christ. Psychiatrists, Schwartz and Gladding define deceptive brain messages as follows: "Any false or inaccurate thought . . . that takes you away from your true goals and intentions in life . . . your true self" (Schwartz and Gladding 2011, 4). Distorted beliefs impact one's identity in Christ. However, formational counseling is a spiritual formational process, which utilizes a prototype of facilitating a God centered atmosphere for individuals to uncover distorted and false beliefs, and process past distressing emotional wounds.

This book highlights formational counseling as an effective tool for care-givers in their ministry of positioning broken people for healing, thus positively impacting their Christian identity. Caregivers in this process assist broken people to correlate knowledge of their deep emotional wounds with an awareness of their dysfunctional behaviors (Wardle 2007, 57). Connecting these two facets of knowledge and awareness is imperative in the healing process. Schwartz and Gladding describes this process as follows:

> After a deceptive brain message arises, you experience
> intensely uncomfortable sensations that can be physical or
> emotional . . . . As a result, you respond in an automatic
> (habitual) way that is ultimately unhelpful or unhealthy
> for you. (Schwartz and Gladding 2011, 11)

Caregivers are very instrumental in assisting the broken person in the process of this connection awareness.

Since most past wounds have never been processed in light of its occurrence with the traumatic event, most people primarily only release, or discuss the facts centering on the event. Therefore, they are unaware of the strong need to process their emotional feelings of struggles attached to such wounds. In an attempt for clarity in understanding these wounds, Wardle developed a simple non-clinical typology of trauma in five categories (Wardle2007, 57). These categories are further discussed below.

Traumatic Wounds of Withholding in Childhood (Wardle 2007), the first in the five categories of trauma, are wounds that occur in one's early life. These wounds occurred in children, whose needs were not attended to by those adults designated as their caretakers. Young children need nurturing and affection that communicate to them significance, in order to create self-assurance in their future life challenges. *Traumatic Wounds of Aggression in Childhood*, the second trauma category, is wounds that were unwarranted in a child's life such as abandonment, physical abuse, verbal and sexual abuse. Wounds of aggression come from the actions of those people who played significant roles in the care of the child in early life.

Traumatic Wounds Caused by Stressful Events (Wardle 2007), the third type of trauma wounds, are the occurrences of life's stressful events that exceed normal life occurrences. *Traumatic Wounds Caused by Betrayal*, the fourth type, are wounds of betrayal resulting from the abuse of power that an authority figure exerted wrongfully in the child's early years. Betrayal wounds damage basic trust in the child, which breeds profound emotional insecurity throughout one's life. *Traumatic Wounds Caused by Long Term Duress*, the fifth and final category in this typology, is trauma wounds of duress. This type of wound is negative stress experienced over a long period of time, which eventually depletes a person's sense of power as a human being. Wardle also encourages us to understand that Jesus experienced and knows the feelings of trauma and is therefore prepared and equipped to meet us in the brokenness of our past (Wardle 2007, 58-68). These five typologies of emotional trauma provide a framework to aid people in categorizing the variety of cruel actions that are familiar to them. The experience of emotional trauma harmfully impacts their identity in Christ.

The Inward Journey of the Caregiver

While caregivers may be educated in various therapeutic counseling disciplines, they must be diligently aware of their own personal emotional journey toward wholeness (Wardle 2007, 121). Caregivers in their ministry of inner healing should also be in an ongoing journey of healing their own emotional wounds. Henri Nouwen notes that as caregivers discern the turmoil and emotionally closed off areas in their own inner lives, they will be less anxious and confused. Thus, they will be converted into capable caregivers ministering to the needs of others (Nouwen 1972, 38). The caregiver more readily assumes a posture of sensitivity, in ministering to others, in his or her personal vulnerability on the ongoing journey of inner-healing. Author, Dan Allender, sums up the importance of our on-going healing process in the following: "To honor the data of life requires that we open ourselves to all the good as well as to what is disconcerting and difficult to face" (Allender 1999, 37). Therefore, our openness in this area, allows for us to receive the person in need with warm enchantment.

As caregivers develop in their ministry of inner healing, they also need to recognize that God provided special endowments (or core longings) of relational blessings to humankind that facilitates their wholeness. These endowments are meant to be provided to a child within an environment of nurturing adults, thereby promoting identity security in the child. Dr. Wardle suggests that the child's parents and significant others are to provide "a safe and secure environment; constant reinforcement of personal worth; repeated messages that the person is valued, unique, and special; unconditional love and acceptance; basic care and nurture; encouragement to grow and develop personal gifts and talents; a pathway to fellowship with God" (Wardle, 2001, 44). The child feeling safe (even when he or she makes mistakes) in its environment will lead to a healthy adulthood.

Yet, on the other hand, most caregivers themselves have experienced emotional trauma that has impacted them. The pain from this trauma is enormous, and leaves many feeling worthless, unfulfilled and unconfident. Furthermore, people who have been deeply emotionally wounded, without healing, will grow to have a distorted belief system about their selves. This belief system results in personal behaviors that are destructive. Therefore, people will assemble a multi-layered mechanism to cope with their upheavals in emotions that drive their dysfunctional behaviors. Dr. Wardle has created a method to define a causal relational effect, which connects one's unhealthy behaviors with one's deep pain and loss. The pain layer is referred to as the first layer of coping defense that symbolizes an individual's response to pain. It may exhibit itself in behaviors such as various addictions, in an attempt to soothe one's painful feelings. The second layer is a protective layer of defense, or a hedge of protection, which encourages the individual to be more on guard and watchful. The third layer, provision, is where the individual attempts to self-provide through, for example, pleasing others for approval. The fourth layer is that of punishment, which fosters anger and the desire to acquire revenge (Wardle 2001, 43-50). It is important for caregivers to be assiduous in attending to their own inner healing of emotional wounds, in order to be effective in their inner healing ministry to others.

A Framework for Structure in the Inner Healing Process

"The caregiver should think of the structures of inner healing as the layers of an onion" (Wardle 2001, 136). A circumstance where the person experiences emotional pain is the outer layer, which is the individual's life situation. Under the life situation is the layer of dysfunctional behaviors, which are unhealthy behavioral reactions to the life situation. The third layer, the emotional upheaval, drives the dysfunctional behaviors in the emotionally wounded. The fourth layer, the lies and distortions or false beliefs in the individual, have been shaped by past unprocessed emotional feelings. The fifth layer is a wound experienced from an emotional traumatic event or even a diminished stressful experience, which has negatively impacted how the individual feels or thinks about him or herself (Wardle 2001, 136-139). Therefore, it is evident from this structure that one's experience of unprocessed emotional traumatic wounds will cause emotional pain. That pain then creates untrue beliefs within the individual about their self, which creates emotional upheavals. Dysfunctional behaviors are attempts to ease the pain within life situations.

"The goal of inner healing prayer is to position people for a transforming encounter with Christ in the places of their deepest pain and greatest dysfunction" (Wardle 2001, 140). Through the ministry of the Holy Spirit, the caregiver positions the emotionally wounded to meet Jesus for healing in the place of the unprocessed wound. Schwartz and Gladding characterizes this process in the following:

> By integrating the view of the Wise Advocate and using insight, awareness, morals, and values to guide your responses and empower you to make choices that are in your long-term best interest. The brain, in contrast, tends to act in an automatic way that ensures momentary survival and a sense of safety. (Schwartz and Gladding 2011, 23)

Coordinating, balancing and integrating one's brain and mind, the wounded is in position for healing. However, it is important to note, that through the Lord's Grace, one's false beliefs are replaced by truth of their identity in Christ. This truth exudes peace and comfort in the individual, in the midst of his or her challenges for further empowerment in life situations (Wardle 2001, 140). With this structure, the wounded individual then has the option to travel on a different pathway, which brings about the desired healing, and also absolutely impacts his or her identity in Christ.

People suffering with emotional wounds may often display reluctance in opening up to others and delving into their past emotional pain. Therefore, caregivers must be prepared to accept this ministry as a journey that is processed over time. Healing is usually not an instantaneous experience. The caregiver who decides to journey with individuals in need of deep emotional healing must be committed to the long-term process of this ministry (Wardle 2007, 79-82). For this reason, caregivers must be equipped with necessary resources to be effective. Subsequently, Dr. Wardle recommends seven resources that caregivers need in the ministry of guiding people through the healing journey of emotional wounds. These resources are discussed below.

A safe place is the first resource needed in the ministry of inner healing. Safe place, according to Dr. Wardle, is "a way that the Spirit communicates truth through a surrendered and sanctified imagination" (Wardle 2007, 83). Our imaginations allow us to have an experience through the intellect of our mind. Gregory Boyd (2004) observes that Western Christians are unaccustomed to the use of their imagination in spiritual affairs. He points out that we do not trust our imagination and think it will remove us from truth, instead of seeing it as useful to facilitating our ability to experience truth (Boyd 2004, 72). Our imagination is actually paramount in how we synthesize all of our thoughts.

Creating an atmosphere that feels safe to wounded people to encounter Jesus is supremely essential for caregivers to achieve. Since wounded people often do not feel safe, it is difficult for them to process past wounds. Wardle expounds on a process that is a Spirit directed prayer exercise utilizing the imagination of the wounded. He explains, "It is not pretending . . . . It is opening the imagination to the Holy Spirit so that He can help one picture in the mind's eye the reality of the Lord's love and care" (Wardle 2007, 83). God created humans with the imagination to experience His Love. Gerald May writes, "In a very intimate, present-centered way, it is indeed possible to quiet our compartmentalizing minds" (May 1992, 200). In a prayerful state, hearts are calm to experience Jesus' presence and His peace.

As we encounter a safe place within our inner being with a surrendered heart and an imagination that is pure, the Holy Spirit can, at that time, impart truth to our souls. Note, this truth will always be in alignment with what is in Scripture which is a confirmation for one's imagination (Wardle 2007, 83-84). The following is an abbreviated version of the safe place exercise:

- *Sit quietly and take several deep breaths.*
- *After a few moments, invite the Holy Spirit to take over your imagination.*
- *Ask the Spirit to create within your mind a safe place where you can meet the Lord.*
- *When ready, tell Jesus how you feel about him. Then ask how he feels about you. He may respond with words or maybe actions. Either way, experience his acceptance and delight.*
- *If you are ready to conclude the exercise, simply spend a few moments in thanks and praise. Take a few deep breaths, letting them out slowly.* (Wardle 2007, 84-85)

This exercise should take place in a supportive environment with a knowledgeable caregiver. During the exercise, the caregiver is attentive to various incorrect images that could derail the wounded person into deception and away from encountering Jesus. Proficiency in this process occurs over time (Wardle 2007, 85). Therefore, patience is a necessary virtue for maturity in this process of experiencing the presence of the Spirit and encountering Jesus.

Support is the second needed resource for caregivers in the passage of healing people with traumatic emotional wounds. The caregiver's desire and dedication to helping people heal is not enough for the healing process to be successful. The wounded person also needs to be in community with other believers for their support, prayers, and recognition. Conscientious caregivers are alert to the third and fourth needed resources. These entail the need for the caregiver to seek permission and obtain an invitation from the individual receiving care. These are vital requests to the wounded person that include their consent to pray and be present with them in their personal space (Wardle 2007, 86-91). The caregiver must be responsive to be encouraging and mindful to make these requests to those in need of help. While it is important for the caregiver to communicate in words, it is notable to point out the views of authors, Brent Bill and Beth Booram regarding this form of communication in the following:

> Words are the primary form of communication we use to nurture our spiritual lives. They happen to be the language of the left brain. However, the left brain cannot experience—God or anything else. The left brain takes meaning from our experiences; the right brain does the experiencing. (Bill and Booram 2012, 12-13)

In order for the wounded to better experience the presence of The Holy Spirit, the intuitive part of the brain must be utilized in the healing process.

Therefore, opening of the senses is the fifth resource recommended by Dr. Wardle for caregivers, which is a right brain exercise. This technique allows for the interactions of right brain movements that provide one the ability to be perceptive and personal. It also categorizes feelings and how one feels about something. The right side of the brain is the source of inspiration and creativeness in humans. Pain and memories of the past that are unprocessed, hinder potential energy that is stored in the right brain. Therefore, through releasing the senses, the wounded person can get in touch with that energy (Wardle 2007, 93). Right brain activities generate an atmosphere for individuals to consciously experience the present moment.

Patience and encouragement are the sixth and seventh resources needed by caregiver in the ministry of inner healing. As David Seamands puts it, "we also need to understand this in order to not judge other people too harshly, but to have patience with their confusing and contradictory behavior" (Seamands 1981, 12). As the caregiver exhibits these virtuous qualities of patience and encouragement, the wounded will experience a feeling being emotionally safe. According to Wardle, ". . . the resources of encouragement and patience are best distributed by a caregiver who . . . is constant in love, strong in faith, and tireless in service to a brother or sister in need" (Wardle 2007, 96). Patience and encouragement are indispensable qualities within caregivers, which aid them in calming the anxious feelings of those experiencing trauma from their past emotional wounds.

As the caregiver plans for the journey of ministry to assist others in their healing, several additional resources are, as well, advocated by Wardle. This journey requires the resource of time commitment that engages formational prayer with an assortment of homework activities for the wounded, outside of the care-giving sessions. Explaining and structuring the process that will be utilized by the caregiver is important to reduce the anxiety of the unknown with individuals needing help. Also, the caregiver's awareness of various spiritual exercises will arm him or her with a mixture of ways of being open in encountering the ministry of The Holy Spirit (Wardle 2007, 97-109). A crucial cognizant theme for caregivers is their willingness to be equipped with these resources in their ministry to position others for inner healing through formational prayer. Author and psychiatrist, Keith Ablow confirms the importance of being well equipped as a caregiver by stating that, "it is my most ambitious attempt to help people . . . face the truth about the past, however uncomfortable, sad, or frightening—and experience the remarkable power that comes from that journey" (Ablow 2007, 7). Subsequently, in due course, the movement toward emotional healing of unprocessed traumatic memories in wounded individuals will positively impact their identity in Christ.

An Eight-Step Strategy Summary to Wardle's Formational Prayer Model

The formational prayer model, developed by Wardle, is a process that progresses in steps for positioning people to encounter Jesus in their deepest emotional pain. This process is made powerful through the ministry of the Holy Spirit to deal with individuals' hurtful and painful wounds, false beliefs, emotional upheavals, and dysfunctional behaviors that are engrained within their inner self (Wardle 2007, 122). The formational prayer model is an effective approach that equips caregivers in facilitating people out of the bondage of emotional pain toward the goal of liberation.

Through the ministry of the Holy Spirit, these steps in the formational prayer model are biblically grounded for aiding the emotionally wounded in experiencing healing. The healing steps are as follows:

> Step One: Establish an atmosphere conducive to the process of formational prayer. Step Two: Provide the necessary support. Step Three: Prioritize safety. Step Four: Position the person before the Lord. Step Five: Encourage the open expression of feelings about struggling with PTSD and other related disorders. Step Six: Ask the Holy Spirit to identify the original source of the emotional upheaval. Step Seven: Help the person tell the story of the traumatic event. Step Eight: Position the person for a new episodic encounter with Jesus. (Wardle 2007, 122-123)

The Lord wants the broken person to experience transformational healing. This process is described by Stephen Seamands in the following: "To bring our wounds to the foot of the cross, we have to walk the road to the cross and choose the way of the cross" (Seamands 2003, 13). Therefore, Wardle's formational prayer model is a strategy for the wounded, to experience such healing, as the wounded person encounters the presence of Jesus at the entry point of his or her wounds. Emotional healing in individuals impacts their ability to receive truth regarding their identity in Christ.

As Christians, we were made in the image of God. Therefore, our self image is replaced with God's image of our identity. Since we are made in God's image to mirror His glory, it is a distortion in our thinking to base our self-worth on values delineated by the secular world. Our thinking regarding ourselves has been depicted in the Bible. It is where we discover that Jesus through His redemptive blood has reconciled humankind back to God. We also can observe through Scripture that Jesus challenges us to be similar to Him. Yet, contemporary views concerning the self lean toward individuals selecting their life choices independent of divine direction. However, humans continuously experience failure in their attempts to live without connections with God (Mintle, 2002, 86). In learning the truth that our image is in God's image, we can comprehend more readily that our true self-worth is revealed in our identity in Christ.

Due to early traumatic emotional wounding leading to faulty thinking patterns, many people's identities have become distorted. Through the ministry of formational counseling, people can receive hope and healing toward experiencing well-being. This approach provides caregivers a method to position hurting people to encounter Jesus at the point of their unprocessed past emotional wounds. It facilitates a journey of transformational healing within hurting individuals toward the definitive self-awareness of knowing their identity in Christ.

CHAPTER FIVE:
BIBLICIAL FOUNDATION OF
CHRISTIAN IDENTITY

In his book, *Learning To Be You: How Our True Identity In Christ Sets Us Free*, David Swanson asserts that people are in a stern identity search to gain knowledge of who they are in this world. However, their search for identity does not include God, our Creator. We need to know, first, how we were formed. Once we have the knowledge of our creation, we can learn our truth. The Gospel of John offers a promise that, ". . . you will know the truth, and the truth will make you free" (Jn. 8:32). Swanson goes on to expound on an experience he encountered through reading a magazine article:

> I came across the story of one-time tennis prodigy Jennifer Capriati. Groomed for stardom from a very young age, she had risen to the top of the tennis world only to be sidelined by repeated injuries, finally being forced to retire . . . . After that I could not figure out who am I? What am I?' (Swanson 2012, 17)

Furthermore, according to Swanson, being unaware of our true identity can facilitate a life of imitation that is artificially stimulated by others. Subsequently, we often experience internal emotional struggles and bewilderment. This disorientation within us can lead to behaviors that result in agonizing outcomes (Swanson 2012, 18). Such outcomes maintain our unceasing search on the path to discovering our awareness of our true identity. Humans want to individually answer the question, "Who am I?"

T. D. Jakes, a prominent pastor based in Dallas, Texas, wrote the forward to Cindy Trimm's book, *The 40 Day Soul Fast: Your Journey To Authentic Living.* He describes in that forward, how humankind has traveled the world, while building the most opulent habitats in which to live and work. In addition, humans have devised ways to protect them from various climates and uninvited creatures. Humans have climbed high mountains, while conquering all sorts of battles and natural disasters. They have discovered electricity, traveled to the outer limits of space, and created medical miracles through science. Yet they continue to search for answers to life's most intrinsic question and mystery, "Who Am I?" However, Jakes points out that God has provided humankind the answers in the bible (Trimm 2011, 15). The question of "Who am I?" seems to be a perennial human question.

Whenever we contemplate the question, "Who am I?" we need to first consider a fundamental truth, and that is, we have been created in God's image (Bridges 2012, 7). It is in the bible, where we find this fundamental truth regarding our creation, including answers to the following questions: "Who Am I?" and "What is my identity?" The bible has many passages expressing that we are God's children, and He has a purpose for His children. Since we are in relationship with God through Jesus Christ, we are redeemed from the curse of *The Fall.* Jesus Christ has fastened God's eternal purpose regarding the children of God (Radmacher, Allen and House 1999, 1441-1442). Even within these few descriptive phrases, we can determine, from a glimpse into the bible, the value God has placed on humanity.

Humankind Created in the Image of God

In Genesis, we read that humankind was created in the image of God: "So God created humankind in his image, in the image of God he created them; male and female he created them" (Gen. 1:27). In this passage, God made both male and female in His own likeness. Humankind is the only creature made in the image of God, as denoted in all biblical accounts (Towner and Sibley 2005). Therefore, humankind's creation is exceptionally significant. St. Augustine (354 – 430 CE) suggests that similar to a seal, the soul of humankind is engraved with the image of God (Moltmann 1993, 237). In fact, God referred to His work as "very good" after he created humankind, as we read in the following: "God saw everything that he had made, and indeed, it was very good" (Gen. 1:31). John MacArthur, biblical scholar, points out that, "What had been pronounced good individually was now called 'very good' collectively. There were no flaws or omissions" (MacArthur 2005, 11). God used the descriptive word "very" to exact an added prominence of importance on how "good" His completed work was after He created humankind.

Additionally, a notable concept according to Nonna Harrison is that, "God's creation of human beings is an expression of his love" (Harrison 2010, 33). Thus, humankind's creation at its core is the enormous love God has for humankind. Biblical professor, Ronald Allen concurs with depicting that God displayed affectionate care in humankind's creation with His act of breathing life into the human being (Radmacher, Allen and House 1999, 8-9). God's very own breadth into humankind has created a notable distinction among and within God's creation. Moreover, Claus Westermann (1909—2000), author and Old Testament scholar, points out the following:

> To be in the image and likeness of God means that human dignity cannot be abrogated by distinctions between groups or sorts of people, that it is inherent in the will of the creator, and that it embraces all. (Westermann 1994, 604)

Humankind was not created by God to be related on the same level as the animal creatures or the plants. They were created as the most outstanding, exceptional and superb of all God's work in creation.

What is more, humankind is not only made in the image of God; humankind's very existence to possess life is totally dependent on God. This is confirmed by the Apostle Paul in Scripture: "For in him we live and move and have our being" (Acts 17:28). The Apostle Paul defines humankind's way of life to be relationally connected and dependent on God (Dunn and Rogerson 2003, 1248). As a result, humankind does not even possess its own life-sustaining power for breathing. Without the breath of life emanating from God, humanity would not have its animation. Thus, in every millimeter of a second is the presence of God in each human being with every breath of air they breathe.

As it is substantiated in the bible, before humankind was created, God articulated, "Let us make humankind in our image, according to our likeness . . " (Gen. 1:26). The word "Us" in this passage refers to "The Triune God" or "The Trinity". Towner and Sibley point out that, "if the godhead is indeed triune in nature, every reference to God in Scripture implies Creator, Christ, and Spirit" (Towner 2005). Therefore, we see an active decisive role of "The Trinity" in the creation of humankind.

Harrison asserts that God the Father, Son and Holy Spirit purposefully and jointly made a decision to create humankind. Yet, as this task is mutually performed, the task is done together as one Triune God (Harrison 2010, 170). Human beings in the image of the Triune God make possible how the psalmist characterizes us as marvelously made, "I praise you, for I am fearfully and wonderfully made" (Ps. 139:14). We have been distinguished by both Judeo and Christian beliefs that each human possesses a spirit, a soul, and a body. These factors in human beings are intricately linked together, and each mysteriously impacts the other (Shaw 2013, 4). Accordingly, this relational connection between the spirit, soul, and body provides humankind a force of significance, only given by God.

Nevertheless, the complete image of God portrayed in humanity is depicted in the personhood of Jesus Christ. The Apostle Paul describes Jesus as follows, "He is the image of the invisible God, the firstborn of all creation; for in him all things in heaven and on earth were created . . ." (Col. 1:15-16). What's more, according to Towner, the "image" and "likeness" of God in humankind allows for a distinction between the natural and the supernatural features that are within human beings. Humankind's invisible abilities such as memory, self-awareness, spirituality and intelligence (to name a few) are in the image of God. Humanity, as well, demonstrates the image of God in the area of emotions and the freewill to make choices in morality, which are qualities not allocated in animals. Therefore, humankind created in the image and likeness of God indicates a uniqueness that is similar to the relationship present within the Triune God (Towner 2005). We can emphatically conclude, humankind is created in the image and likeness of God, the Creator of the universe.

Being created in God's image, humankind is placed in a separate category from the animals that God created. Therefore, humankind has a dual relationship with God, which includes both being reliant and answerable to God (Bridges 2012, 7). The Psalmist states that, "The eyes of all look to you, and you give them their food in due season. You open your hand, satisfying the desire of every living thing" (Ps. 145:15-16). While this passage is about the animal creatures, the theme of reliance on God is also indicative of humankind (Bridges 2012, 7). Even though humankind is superior to the animal kingdom, both species rely on God for their earthly existence.

Nonetheless, God created humankind in relationship to Himself, and instructed them to take care of everything that He created on earth. In creating humankind, God authorized them to be in charge of all His creation. He created them in His image. It is reported that in the ancient world, the core of a thing was in its image (Walton, Matthews and Chavalas 2000, 29). No one individual can be thought of, as less, or more, than another human being. Accordingly, "Every person, with no distinction of race, nation, or gender bears God's image in precisely the same degree . . . . If one person can be viewed or treated as being less than the image of God, then all of us can, and eventually will" (Green 1996). Thus, humankind symbolizes the very fundamental nature of God, the Creator of the entire universe.

While God created humanity from the earth, according to Millard Erickson, God calls humankind in totality, a soul. As a result, there is not a sharp distinction between humankind's body and soul. Further, an important point is that in Hebrew, a person is not restricted to the soul, but is the whole of the person (Erickson 1995, 163). Unlike the animal kingdom, humankind was created by God with moral principles. Bridges declares that humankind has the wherewithal to distinguish between what is right, and what is wrong (Bridges 2012, 13). This knowledge provides humankind the ability to discern the difference between doing as told, or not doing as told.

God created a moral universe, and gave human beings the privilege of possessing a free will. Nevertheless, humans may choose to use their freedom of choice to commit wrong (Brown 2012, 305). All the same, humans were created by God with a liberated will to make choices. It is depicted throughout the bible, that God's relationship with humankind is one of human freedom. This is evident in the following Scripture passage that describes an occasion where a group of people are given the privilege of a free will choice:

> But if your heart turns away and you do not hear, but are
> led astray to bow down to other gods and serve them, I
> declare to you today that you shall perish; . . . . [19] I call
> heaven and earth to witness against you today that I have
> set before you life and death, blessings and curses. Choose
> life so that you and your descendants may live, loving the
> LORD your G God . . . . (Deut. 30:18-19)

While this is one passage that demonstrates humankind being offered the freedom to choose according to their own free will, there are other passages that offer similar choices, for example: Joshua 24:15; Ezekiel 18:30-32; Matthew 7:24; and Luke 14:28. Often in Scripture, such as in the above passage (Deut. 30:15-19), we see God encouraging His people, including Moses and the prophets, to perform that which is right and not to do what is evil or wrong (Harrison 2010, 12). God has created humankind in His image with the privilege and capacity of a free will. This passage also demonstrates how these people made the choice of life instead of death, which is in agreement with their leader and prophet, Moses (House and Mitchell 2007, 85). People were clearly provided appropriate information that God's love and desire was for them to choose life.

Humankind's Fall from Relationship with God

It is imperative to examine humankind's creation, within the framework of how humankind succumbed to the fall. This examination will provide a structure to comprehend a complete representation of the importance surrounding the fall to our identity in Christ (Andersen 2000, 28). In Genesis, we see that God not only formed humankind from the dust of the earth, but He ". . . breathed into his nostrils the breath of life; and the man became a living being" (Gen. 2:7). In view of this Scripture verse, Andrew Louth explains that God puts humans in a state to share His own grace so that they would recognize their likeness to God's likeness. Humankind was granted by God, a magnitude of honor, which is even above the heavens, sun and stars. There is no other creation of God possessing such honor in the heavenly bodies, and created in the very image of God (Louth 2001, 51). God provided humankind a status of significance above all of creation.

God was very pleased with His creation of humankind. He provided life into humankind with His very own breath (Gen. 2:7). However, the first two created human beings became the first victims of

47

identity theft by Satan, which affected all humankind thereafter. Satan persuaded Adam and Eve that their identity was not what God said it to be. Adam's first error was that he did not contest Satan's allegations regarding God's Word (Shaw 2013, 2). Adam and Eve continued on a path of disobedience. This path led them to make a devastating decision, which was to disobey God and eat the forbidden fruit.

While in the beginning humankind's soul was in adherence to God's authority, humankind's earthly body also was in compliance to the authority of God. However, Satan's persuasive tactics caused humankind to become rebellious. The rebellion creates internal conflict within humankind's mind and body (Aquinas 1951, 327). The Apostle Paul describes this conflict as follows, ". . . I see in my members another law at war with the law of my mind, making me captive to the law of sin that dwells in my members" (Rom. 7:23). Paul concludes that, this internal struggle precipitates into sinful captivity within the body.

This behavior of Adam and Eve resulted in their fatal downfall, or the fall. We read in Genesis, ". . . she took of its fruit and ate; and she also gave some to her husband, who was with her, and he ate" (Gen. 3:6). Adam and Eve did not adhere to God's boundaries, and they refused His limitations. Satan, on the other hand, tempted them with questions of doubt and unbelief toward God's goodness, His Truth and His Word. This unbelief caused Adam and Eve's defiance against God. They became their own lawmakers against the ruler ship of God (Waltke 2001, 46). They wanted to elevate and position their selves up, to be on the same level with God.

Moreover, Adam and Eve became envious of God's status. They desired to be on an equal level with God, even though they were created by God in God's image. So they ate the forbidden fruit from the tree of knowledge of good and evil. With a cataclysmic abrupt disaster, God's image in humankind was broken (Kirwan 1984, 78). This broken image impacted the identity Adam and Eve within themselves.

When God called out to Adam in the garden, Adam hid from God, in fear. Adam acknowledged God's call, in that, he said, "I heard you in the garden and I was afraid because I was naked. And I hid" (Gen. 3:10, The Message Bible). Now that Adam had knowledge of good and evil, he experienced shame, which caused him to hide, and he became alienated from God.

The Apostle Paul points out that, ". . . all die in Adam . . ." (1 Cor. 15:22). The consequence of Adam's behavior was death for all humans. Since all humans came from Adam, they also took on the label of being made sinners. However, Christ did not bear the label of a sinner, because Christ did not come from Adam. Christ descended from God. Therefore, each individual enters earth with a sinful character. Consequently, all humankind is positioned before God through only two persons, that of Adam, and that of Christ (Bridges 2012, 18). God's arrangement with humankind is with Adam and Christ.

God's Plan of Reconciliation to Humankind

The question, "Who am I?", that we as human beings frequently ponder, was answered by King David in the words that we are "a sinner" (Ps. 51:5). MacArthur writes that, "David acknowledged that his sin was not God's fault in any way" (MacArthur 2005, 634). David admitted the reason for his sin was his fault do to his own fallen self. "David, like you and me, was represented by Adam in the garden, and through the disobedience of Adam, David was made a sinner" (Bridges 2012, 19). However, the Apostle Paul declares good news for humankind by stating, ". . . so all will be made alive in Christ" (1 Cor. 15:22). MacArthur expounds on this passage as follows, "Adam who through his sin brought death on the whole human race, was human. So was Christ, who by His resurrection brought life to the race" (MacArthur 2005, 1606).

God has provided a mechanism to close the gap of humankind's alienation from Him through His Son, Jesus Christ. "God is faithful; by him you were called into the fellowship of his Son, Jesus Christ our Lord" (1 Cor. 1:9). Author, N. T. Wright declares the following:

> Paul clearly believes Jesus is the one through whom his people are reconciled to the creator, through whom therefore is being brought about the dawn of the new creation . . . . (Wright 1993, 131)

As a result, God wants to demonstrate His commitment to humankind through humankind's communion and companionship with Christ. Accordingly, "Our calling is grounded in and culminates in the communion with Christ which has been given to us" (Scheele 1998, 351). Humans have been given by God sacred fellowship privileges through Christ, which no other earthly species has the privilege to enjoy.

Seamands suggests the Trinitarian personhood conveyed in Genesis is fundamental to comprehending the fellowship and image of God (*Imago Dei*) in humankind. Therefore, when we see a person, we see a being made in the image of God (Seamands 2005, 35). God created humans to be like Him, and to be in relationship with Him. However, the fall of humanity, through Adam's sinful behavior, interrupted humankind's relationship with God.

Despite the fact that the Apostle Paul stated humans were dead in their wrongs, God provided humankind a transformational plan of adoption and reconciliation. Paul writes "You were dead through the trespasses and sins in which you once lived . . ." (Eph. 2:1). MacArthur points out this verse reveal to us that, ". . . sinfulness . . . from which believers have been redeemed indicates the realm or sphere in which unregenerate sinners exist" (MacArthur 2005, 1686). Nevertheless, God has a plan for humans' restoration that leads them back to a right relationship with Him. Neil Andersen asks the question: "What is God's plan for transforming us from being in Adam to being in Christ" (Anderson 2000, 46)? Jesus said, "Very truly, I tell you no one can see the kingdom of God without being born from above" (John 3:3). Robert Gundry depicts the following:

> What's meant is that birth from the Spirit produces a human spirit (with a small "s" don't make a distinction" capitalization versus non capitalization being a matter of interpretation since ancient manuscripts don't make a distinction), because human beings have a human spirit quite apart from birth above. What's meant is that birth from the Spirit produces people inhabited by the Holy Spirit . . . . (Gundry, Robert H. 2010, 360)

As Anderson concludes, Spiritual birth produces Spiritual life, which is a transformational process (Anderson 2000, 46).

Throughout generations, the process of transformation has commonly been called the "New Birth". When we are "born again", our soul becomes one with God through Christ, similar to the way Adam was one with God before the fall (Anderson 2000, 46). Therefore, to be aware of this transformation is to be aware that one's true identity is rooted in who one is in Christ. The phrase "New Birth" or "born again" comes from God who allows humankind to become His children when they place their trust in Jesus Christ (MacArthur 2005, 1357). The mystery of the new birth allows humankind to be called God's children through identity in Jesus Christ.

Spiritual rebirth, as noted in Scripture, facilitates a transformational process, whereby Christians become significant people, who are purpose driven to declare God's works to others. In 1 Peter 2:9, we read, "But you are a chosen race, a royal priesthood, a holy nation, God's own people, in order that you may proclaim the mighty acts of Him who called you out of darkness into His marvelous light" (1 Peter 2:9). Gundry describes this passage as the following, "Christians have replaced Israel as the nation consecrated by God to himself; and it is this consecration that makes them a nation despite their ethnic diversity" (Gundry 2010, 943). The New Testament describes God's people as a "holy priesthood to offer spiritual sacrifices acceptable to God through Jesus Christ" (Elwell and Comfort 2001, 1073). This passage describes Christians as chosen people, who are given a high status of royalty by God, Himself.

In God blessing Christians with such a high status, we bring Him glory through our reflection of His image within our personhood. Scripture refers to us as an earthly light. "You are the light of the world" (Matt. 5:14). According to Robert Gundry, Christians enlighten the full earth similar to how the sun radiates in the entire earth (Gundry 2010, 17). Our light that shines from within us glorifies God our Creator. When human beings live out a life daily that reflects God's image, they carry out their true significance (Shaw 2013, 6). Therefore, we find that the significance of our true identity commences with us yielding to God's love. Biblical scholar, H. Wayne House points out that Christians do not have an innate light but a reflective light that glorifies God. As we continue our connection to Christ, God's light reflects through us and is seen by others in our environment (Radmacher, Allen and House 1999, 1148). As we walk in our Christian identity, God's light reflects in our lives and seen by others, who will in due course glorify God.

The Apostle Paul further explains in Ephesians, how God's enormous love for humankind is the substance of His plan of redemption. In the bible, redemption can cover an assortment of connotations. One dictionary definition of redemption is "liberation" or "release or freedom on payment of a price" (Douglas and Tenney 1987, 849). Hence, redemption through the work of Christ affords us forgiveness, which is a debt cancellation of humankind's responsibility of payment for sin. "Here is the Lamb of God who takes away the sin of the world" (John 1:29). Therefore, as Robert Gundry puts it, Jesus is not an ordinary lamb, but the lamb that is provided by God. Customarily sinners presented their individual sacrificial lambs as an offering to God. However, in this instance God has reversed that order, in that He, God offers Jesus as the sacrificial lamb to erase the world's transgression (Gundry 2010, 352). Consequently, the work of Christ allows God to remove our sin from our record. "I am He who blots out your transgressions for my own sake, and I will not remember your sins" (Is. 43:25). MacArthur portrays this verse as an elevated position of grace in the Old Testament, without concession to God's Holiness, regardless of Israel's sinful behavior. Therefore, God would transmit this redemptive plan through the labor of Jesus Christ (MacArthur 2005, 812). By this means, our sins are not held adjacent to us.

According to Michael Gorman, biblical professor, "God has an eternal plan, a mystery, which has now been revealed: to gather up all things in Christ" (Gorman 2004, 516). This eternal redemption plan provides reconciliation of humankind back to Him through His Son, Jesus Christ. The Apostle Paul reveals this plan in Ephesians 1:3-14:

> Blessed be the God and Father of our Lord Jesus Christ, who has blessed us in Christ with every spiritual blessing in the heavenly places, just as he chose us in Christ before the foundation of the world to be holy and blameless before him in love. He destined us for adoption as his children through Jesus Christ, according to the good pleasure of his will, to the praise of his glorious grace that he freely bestowed on us in the Beloved. In him we have redemption through his blood, the forgiveness of our trespasses, according to the riches of his grace that he lavished on us. With all wisdom and insight he has made known to us the mystery of his will, according to his good pleasure that he set forth in Christ as a plan for the fullness of time, to gather up all things in him, things in heaven and things on earth. In Christ we have also obtained an inheritance, having been destined according to the purpose of him who accomplishes all things according to

his counsel and will, so that we, who were the first to set our hope on Christ, might live for the praise of his glory. In him you also, when you had heard the word of truth, the gospel of your salvation, and had believed in him, were marked with the seal of the promised Holy Spirit; this is the pledge of our inheritance toward redemption as God's own people, to the praise of his glory. (Eph. 1:3-14)

The New Testament book of Ephesians depicts the ideal church as Christ's body (Schaff 2006, 783). Therefore, as church members, each Christian's identity is vitally rooted in the body of Christ. Also, authors Bromiley and Harrison denote, "Ephesians grounds the manner of Christian life in the saving work of Christ and the ministry of the Spirit" (Bromiley and Harrison 1982, 187). This Ephesians passage provides information to Christians concerning their belonging and inclusion into God's family.

Ephesians 1:3-14 was a letter written to convert the thoughts of Christians, regarding their identity as people of God, through a frame of mind that initially entails worship. Gombis helps us to understand that some scholars have emphasized these verses were comprised, in a way, to impact how Christians should view their purpose pertaining to God redeeming humankind back to Himself. This context of worship helped the early Christians to rejoice as God's distinctively blessed people. They also were encouraged to remember that God is above all creation. Therefore, humans could worship knowing they were especially designated to connect God to the world (Gombis 2010, 67). The Apostle Paul wanted to impact the identity of Christians through providing them knowledge that God has redeemed His creation. Despite their minority status during the first century, Christians were aware they were at the center of God's plan. The words of the Apostle Paul in this passage of Ephesians (Eph. 1:3) conferred on them an assurance of belonging to God through Jesus

Christ. He, Jesus Christ, is above all powers (Witherington 2007, 237). This knowledge further grounded their identity in Christ.

According to Martin, ". . . the 'spiritual blessings' mentioned in Ephesians 1:3 are neither otherworldly, nor abstract. These 'spiritual blessings' are promises for and changes the flesh-and-blood people of the church" (Martin 1994, 3). The Apostle Paul is rejoicing and giving thanks about God our Father/Creator and Jesus our Christ/Redeemer. Author and noted seminary professor, Anthony Hoekema (1913-1988) points out that, "Union with Christ begins with God's pre-temporal decision to save his people in and through Jesus Christ" (Hoekema 1989, 44). Highlighted also in this passage (Eph. 1:3-14) is that God in Christ, which is outside of human comprehension, chose us for adoption and redemption before the world's foundation was even formed. In Christ, all God's purposeful plans for humankind are under the authority of Christ (Durken 2009, 605). Since Jesus performed the work of redemption for humankind, we are the recipients of all Spiritual blessings. Ephesians (Eph. 1:7) also directs us toward the disorder that is seen in the universe that has caused humans to be alienated from God. Yet, from the text, we see the affirmation of peace and harmony toward humankind from God through Christ (Barnard 2009, 168). Albeit, God's redemption plan for humankind is in Jesus Christ.

Our painstaking exploration for an answer to the question "Who am I?" can cease. It no longer needs to be asked, because God has provided us the answer to this puzzle in the bible. As David Swanson further confirms, the excellent benefit of the bible includes provisions for the following: (1) to direct us to our true identity in Christ; (2) to have valor to walk in that identity; and (3) to subdue our internal tensions that come when we are hindered in functioning in the prior two provisions. As a result, God's answer is initially made known in Ephesians (Eph. 1:5) regarding our predestination for adoption by God through Jesus Christ, which is God's pleasure and will (Swanson 2012, 23). We are God's children through the process of adoption. As noted by Michael Gorman, "Scripture calls God's people 'the children of Israel', with God as their father who blesses and protects them" (Gorman 2004, 507). The adoption process allows us to be identified as children of God.

Throughout the bible, the matter of identity is presented. This elevation of identity, as an important facet of humankind, is evident in the biblical identity of Israel's population. We see represented in various Scriptures (for example, Rom. 12:1-2; Cols. 3:1-4; James 1:27) the early church's identity. In fact, as Douglas and Tenney puts it, the first century Christians were not concerned about their individual names, because their primary focus was with the Name of Jesus Christ (Douglas and Tenney 1987, 210). Hence, as a believer in the New Testament, we must be conscious of our new identity in Christ. As the adopted children of God in Christ, we are recipients of all the fortunate rights that come with inclusion in the family of God (Jn. 1:12). Therefore, we are not developing into God's children. Each individual has already been processed into God's family as a child of God. Thus, the answer to the question of "who am I?" is, "I am a child of God" (Swanson 2012, 23). These truths internalized in our hearts will transform how we see ourselves, because our identity comes from a loving God, The Father.

The Apostle Paul's Model of His Identity in Christ

We can then proceed to identify ourselves with Scripture using the Apostle Paul as a model in how he identified himself on numerous occasions. Paul articulated things about himself in relationship to Christ. Furthermore, as Lloyd-Jones reports, the Apostle Paul declared himself in several instances as an apostle, servant, minister, or bond-slave of Christ. In particular, the introductions in his letters declared his relationship to Christ, and explained his existence because of Christ (Lloyd-Jones 1979, 19). Paul was very much grounded in his identity in Christ. This is evident in his words saying,

> And it is no longer I who live, but it is Christ who lives
> in me. And the life I now live in the flesh I live by faith
> in the Son of God, who loved me and gave Himself for
> me. (Gal. 2:20)

Douglas and Tenney point out that, "God loves the world as a whole . . . as well individuals in it, in spite of the sinfulness and corruption of the human race" (Douglas and Tenney 1987, 603). Paul considered it imperative to live not by faith in his own understanding, but by faith in Christ Jesus.

The Apostle Paul illustrates for us how he was transformed into a new order of identity. He describes himself as dead to the old order of things, and alive to unification with Jesus Christ (Hahn and Mitch 2010, 334). As a result, our Christian identity is impacted through our identity and union with Jesus Christ. Conversely, Paul exhorts the Christians in Rome to understand the renovation of one's identity alteration originates through the regeneration of their intellect. He confirms this experiential process as follows:

> I appeal to you therefore, brothers and sisters, by the mercies
> of God, to present your bodies as a living sacrifice, holy
> and acceptable to God, which is your spiritual worship.
> Do not be conformed to this world, but be transformed
> by the renewing of your minds, so that you may discern
> what is the will of God— what is is good and acceptable
> and perfect. For by the grace given to me I say to everyone
> among you not to think of yourself more highly than you
> ought to think, but to think with sober judgment, each
> according to the measure of faith that God has assigned.
> (Rom. 12:1-3)

Therefore, in Christ we are to submit ourselves as living offerings to God. In this practical way of life, we do not do the accepted thing outwardly if it contradicts our inward beliefs. This behavior is a result of a mind change, or a renewed way of thinking, which comes about through meditating on Scripture and the Holy Spirit. Ultimately, the goal is for Christians to conclude they are nothing in themselves alone. God's grace provides them favor to fulfill their purpose in the call God has given us (MacArthur 1982, 1544). Paul's emphasis is on the importance of the intellect, as the initial step, toward transformational change into the identity of Christ.

Hence, this transformational change in our identity in Christ connects us relationally to our God, our Heavenly Father. Accordingly, authors Reiss and Moshe point out, "To be human and to be in the image of God is not separable" (Reiss and Moshe 2011). Therefore, we can conceive the transcendence of God's image into humankind. God has bequeathed upon humankind the ability to characterize Himself in the world. Subsequently, humankind's purpose is to symbolize God's image within the world (Grenz 2004, 139). This transformational identity change allows for the manifestation of God's image in humankind, and displayed within the world.

CHAPTER SIX:
THEOLOGICAL FOUNDATION
OF CHRISTIAN IDENTITY

The biblical foundation of this book points out that God created humans in relationship to Himself and to His creation. Therefore, the theological basis regarding humankind's Christian identity requires discussion of the following: humans' alienation from God, humans' redemption and reconciliation to God.

Humankind's Creation in the Image of God

Humankind's creation in the image of God is not to be compared with a mirror type image, or a prototype image. Humans are created in the image of God, and in His perfect love for them. Their consciousness of this love will produce an outward display of God's glory (McFarland 2009, 133). God's Love in humans creates t their ability to feel affection for God, and the capacity to comprehend God's Love for them. This Love God has for humankind is evident in His creation. In the observation of all creation, we only see that the human species was created in the very image of God. Being created in the image of God, humans are made to be like God and represent God on earth (Grudem 1994, 442). Humans' spiritual, body and mental wholeness take place inwardly, as humans view themselves in the image of God.

Humans' perception of God's creation establishes not only their view of themselves, but also their view of God. Paul Jewet argues the following:

> Our understanding of creation determines not only how we as Christians understand God and the world, but also how we understand ourselves . . . . My creation is not simply something I say about myself but something God says to me . . . . I find the beatitude of my being in him and thereby the dignity of [my] being as human. (Jewett 1991, 503)

Each person's individuality, uniqueness, and significance derive from belonging to God, our Creator. Therefore, we are here in the world at the pleasure and express desire of God, Himself.

Humankind's Alienation from God

In God's creation of humans to be like Him, man and woman were given dominion over everything. God created people and gave them the responsibility to care for all His earthly creations. He also gifted them to have possession of His very image (Walton, Matthews and Chavalas 2000, 29). However, the first humans, Adam and Eve, made a decision to disobey God, which caused their downfall and alienation from God. This alienation resulted in sin as a consequence of the fall. In their disobedience to God's Word, Adam and Eve rebelled against God and His goodness (Douglas and Tenney 1987, 342). They refused to submit to God's authority, but wanted to be equal with God. Their quest for equality with God is demonstrated in their sinful disobedience. The fact that they did not follow God's instruction indicates sin or rebellion to God, including

His Word. Sinful behavior deforms God's image in humankind internal being, thereby resulting in humankind's relational separation from God.

Stanley Grenz (1950-2005) author and theologian, categorizes sin in the following four metaphors: (1) Alienation, which not only inhibits humankind relationship with God, but prevents relationship with others and creation itself; (2) Condemnation or sin's judgment on humankind, who were created to walk in the image of God's Holiness; (3) Enslavement, or a lack of freedom, due to humankind's inability to live the life that God had ordained at the time of creation; (4) Depravity, which is humankind's lack of strength to change their sin situation (Grenz 1994, 207-212). It is important to note, that sin thwarts humankind's relationship with God, internally, with others and with God's created world. As noted by L. Gregory Jones, author and theology professor, human beings are created by God for communion with God, other human beings and all of God's creation. He further points out, that in order for humankind to learn who they belong to; humankind needs both God and community. Furthermore, according to Jones, humankind's interpersonal relationships permit the execution of humankind's purpose for the vital purpose of God's Kingdom (Jones 1995, 61). Thus, sin harmfully impacts humankind's identity in Christ.

Additionally, the results of sin, according to Grenz, have negatively directly impacted humankind's behavior and way of existing even in their current life situations (Grenz 1994, 207). Sin distorts humankind's mental abilities, which results in behaviors not conducive to optimal livelihoods. Thomas Oden, systematic theologian, echoes that sin impedes humanity's need for a repentant heart, because sin causes emotional brokenness, and produces internal dissimilarity. This internal struggle in humankind affects their identity awareness pertaining to who one is, and with how the individual should personify themselves (Oden 1987, 79). Sin disfigures human beings identity in Christ. Millard Erickson, author and theologian describes sin as not only wrong behavior, but an inner desire to do wrong behaviors that alters and distorts one's character (Erickson 2001, 189). If one has the desire for wrong, one's behavior or acting out of those desires will follow. However, L. Gregory Jones, sums sin's results succinctly, and that is, sin prevents humankind from experiencing a new life in Christ Jesus (Jones 1995, 11). Consequently, sin hinders people from the freedom to experience God's unconditional love through Humankind's Redeemer, Jesus Christ.

God's Plan of Redemption and Reconciliation to Humankind

God always pursues us, because of His colossal love for humankind. Abraham Heschel points out that God has been portrayed as being more interested and involved in the affairs of humankind, more than He is with eternal affairs. God's mind is continuously preoccupied with humankind (Heschel 1962, 6). Humankind constantly occupies the mind of God. The plan of redemption and reconciliation is eternal according to Millard Erickson. While a sequential time configuration is not believed necessary in God's plan, a logical order of events are significant to God's eternal plan. For example, according Erickson, the passion of Christ was a decision by God before the historical Jesus appeared on earth. God is at liberty to select His actions. Therefore, God's intention is independent of external fortitude or any internal persuasive rationale (Erickson 2001, 122). God's plan is grounded in His Holiness that will not be amended. As Grenz puts it, since creation God has exerted a creation to fulfill His plan, which included a plan of reconciling humankind back to Himself. God is not seeking humankind's condemnation (Grenz 1994, 244).

Since creation, God has been in a covenantal relationship with humankind. Michael Horton, author and theology professor, reminds us that even the fall was unable to destroy God's covenantal relationship with humanity. God continues this relationship with humankind through His plan of redemption. Therefore, God in Christ has redeemed and reconciled humankind back to Himself as His adopted children (Horton 2011, 386). In the adoption process, God makes humankind members of His family. This adoption is made possible through God's redemptive plan of reconciliation through Christ. The person Jesus Christ, who knew God, and was God in human flesh, completed an absolutely sacrificial act in His death on the Cross. His rising from that death provided the connection between humankind and God's holiness (Willard 2010, 85). Such a sacrificial behavior on the part of Jesus Christ demonstrates Love beyond human comprehension and intellectual capacity.

God's goal, according to Grudem, is to have humans pattern their lives in the likeness and moral character of Christ. In this knowledge, we now can understand that throughout our lives, we can continuously mature into the resemblance and image of God (Grudem 1994, 445). Adam failed in maintaining his image in God, along with his covenantal relationship with God. Yet, God has restored all of what was lost to humankind through Jesus Christ. Thus, humanity took on historical substance in the personhood of Jesus Christ. However, Volf informs us that Christ is distinct from humankind, because Christ's identity has a twofold relationship. This twofold relationship is comprised of being God the Son, to God the Father; and at the same time, being fully human in relationship to humankind. For that reason, each individual is formed as a person in Christ, resulting in them being unified with God (Volf 1998, 85). It is the personhood of Jesus that provides humanity reconciliation with, and restoration back to, God.

Since all of humankind has been created in the image of God, it is imperative for us, as Christians, to release any false beliefs about our self-identity. These false beliefs are predicated on the sin that entered the earth, and distorted our true identity. Such distortion causes us to alienate ourselves from God. According to L. Gregory Jones, God looks for relationship with humankind through reconciliation, because of His covenantal bond with human beings (Jones 1995, 107). A plan of redemption for us has been created by God through Jesus Christ. And this plan has allowed all of humankind to be reconciled back to God in right covenantal relationship.

CHAPTER SEVEN:
HISTORICAL FOUNDATION
OF CHRISTIAN IDENTITY

A story is told about a man helping his uncle in an old wheat grinding mill during the early years of the twentieth century. The uncle managed a farm where a number of African-American sharecropper farmers resided. As the man aided his uncle one day, a small child, the daughter of a sharecropper, entered the mill and stayed near the door. When the uncle saw the child, he harshly addressed her inquiring what she wanted. The child mildly responded, "My mammy say send her fifty cents." The uncle responded, "I'll not do it, now you run on home." As the child replied, "Yas sah," she did not move. The uncle proceeded in his work not noticing that the child did not leave. When he looked up, and saw her still there, he threatened to strike her with a switch, to which the young girl replied, "Yas sah," without any movement. By this time, the uncle was furious, stopped his work, and took a barrel stave as he moved toward the girl with a very stern face.

The man became afraid his angry uncle would kill this little girl. The man was aware at this time in American history; African American children were not to defy the ruling population in that region of America. However, when the uncle moved to where the girl stood, she hastily stepped forward one step, looked up into his eyes, and shouted as loud as she could,

"My Mammy's got to have that fifty cents!" The uncle stopped, and for a minute just looked at her. Slowly he put the barrel stave down, and he placed his hand in his pocket taking out a half dollar. As the little girl took the money, she slowly backed toward the door. She did not remove her eyes from looking at the man she had maintained to triumph over.

Once the girl had left, the uncle appeared numb, and he sat down staring out the window into space for several minutes. He contemplated in amazement over what had happened. The man telling this true story revealed he also was in awe over what he observed in seeing his response. According to Hill, "his uncle loses his fierceness and became as docile as a lamb" (Hill 2003, 8).

The above story provides a metaphor of faith in action grounded in commitment. The child's commitment to her mother propelled her to persist with an undeniable faith that she would receive fifty cents. In a similar spirit of commitment to that of this child, there are recorded in history many examples of people who have acted out of their commitment to God in their Christian identity regardless of hindrances, difficulties, or even the ultimate, death itself.

Documented historically, as W.H.C. Frend points out, Christians proved their commitment to Christ by being severely challenged in their faith. As some were thrown to wild animals, they were seen praying on their knees as they gave God thanks for His love to them. What was so significant about these martyrs? They could have forfeited death by offering up sacrifices to idols, or to the Roman emperors. However, many were as the second-century Christian Bishop Polycarp (80-167 CE) of Smyrna, who was martyred and said "I cannot deny Him, who has been so faithful to me all these years" (Frend 1984, 182). It is reported soldiers put spears in his side as his body was in flames. The blood from his body put out some of the flames, but the soldiers rekindled the fire until Polycarp's body burned to death (Frend 1984, 182). While this is only a snapshot captured historically, many others have demonstrated similar great commitment to, and faith in their identity in Christ.

Therefore, the historical foundation of impacting Christian Identity reflects discussion on the following significant question: Historically, how has the church assisted the spiritual formation of its members in their Christian identity experientially through relationship, instruction, and various disciplines?

The Spiritual Formation of Church Members through Relationship

The church, historically, has essentially nurtured individual Christian identity through relational experiences among its membership. The word, "church," is derived from the Greek word, "ekklesia" or "ecclesia" meaning an "assembly" (Douglas and Tenney 1987, 218). Hodgson and King provide a broader definition of ecclesia in the following:

> Ecclesia is a transfigured mode of human community, comprised of a plurality of peoples and cultural traditions, founded upon the life, death, and resurrection of Christ, constituted by the redemptive presence of God as Spirit, . . . and in which is actualized a universal reconciling love that liberates from sin, alienation, and oppression. (Hodgson and King 1994, 271)

Therefore, the church consists of a community of people, who are formed in the centrality of the life, death, and resurrection of Jesus Christ.

Early historical church communities established a process of spiritual formation, according to authors Blast, Duhaime and Turcotte, through both Christian instruction and spiritual disciplines. This included learning the Creed, The Prayer of Jesus (often referred to as "The Lord's Prayer"), and included various other teachings from the Old Testament. However, the formalization of this process was not fully active within the church until approximately the fourth and fifth centuries. The process of becoming a person with a unique and distinguishable identity as a Christian was not a speedy process, nor was it a rapid one-step procedure (Blast, Duhaime, and Turcotte 2002, 309-310). The church stressed that Christian conversion was a process.

Historically, according to Saunders, spiritual formation can first be described as the Lordship of Jesus Christ being the center of attention within the early church. Jesus was the icon for representation of Christian faith and application for practical living, including the primary object of devotion. Spiritual formation in the early church also was very focused on the mission of Christianity, which was to proclaim the gospel. Another noted point of spiritual formation in the early church is that this process took place largely within the church community. Spiritual formation was nurtured within the community of the church to construct and erect the body of Christ as a communal life together within community (Saunders 2002, 155-177). The work of spiritual formation was not to be discerned solely in an individualistic style, but within community.

In the writings of Blast, Duhaime and Turcotte, we see that the church's early Christians dwelled in two social worlds. They lived in the world of the Roman Empire, as they simultaneously received instructions from the church on how to be good adherents to *the way of Jesus* (Blast, Duhaime and Turcotte 2002, 441-442). The word "Christian," at that time, was a label given them by the world's majority population to distinguish them as a people who separated themselves from the majority population (Blast, Duhaime and Turcotte 2002, 441-442). Nonetheless, these Christians created their own self identity as followers of Jesus Christ.

While the term "Christian" according to Blast, Duhaime and Turcotte, was designated as a term of shame by the majority, it became a badge of honor by the early Christians. Therefore, during the trials and persecutions of Christians in the second and third centuries, the Christians would make a straightforward confession of their Christian identity by proclaiming: "I am a Christian." These Christian proclamations had a twofold meaning: (1) a badge of honor; and (2) an expression that could be punishable by death (Blast, Duhaime and Turcotte 2002, 441-442). The identity of the early believers in their Christian faith was an actual concrete commitment, which was demonstrated even in the face of death.

Spiritual Formation through Instruction and Various Disciplines

Throughout this period of the early church, many pagans converted to Christianity. As a result, the early church leaders felt a strong need to incorporate a structured program of instruction and disciplines for practical living within its community. Therefore, the second and third centuries saw a very rigorous standard of requirements for converts seeking to be baptized into Christianity. It is important to note, this meticulous standard was much more stringent in the second and third centuries compared to baptismal requirements for new converts in the first century. The first century apostles were elated to baptize people in the initial period of being newly acquainted with new converts (Hill 2011, 98). Subsequently, second-century Christians were mandated to certain beliefs and behavioral standards before receiving baptism as a Christian.

We see in the writings of *The Didache of the Twelve Apostles* during the early second century, many of the disciplines and teachings used to impact the spiritual formation of the Christian community. Bart Ehrman provides a synopsis of the early church's formational instruction in the following:

> *The Didache of the Twelve Apostles* (*didache* literally means "the teaching") . . . it (a) preserves our earliest account of how the early Christians practice their rituals of baptism and the Eucharist, (b) discloses the kinds of prayers that early Christians said, (c) indicates the days on which they fasted, . . . (Ehrman 2004, 447-449)

69

Continuing through the second and third centuries, early church fathers moved further toward expounding on all Scriptures in light of the person of Christ.

Clement of Alexandria taught from 190 until 203 CE at the catechetical school at Alexandria, that Scripture has two meanings, similar in comparison to the structure of the human body. He taught that Scripture, like the human body, has a literal part as well as a soul or spiritual part. Clement emphasized that the spiritual, or the hidden part of Scripture, is its most important aspect (Klein, Blomberg and Hubbard 2004). Utilizing metaphors in teaching abstract concepts provided the listeners a practical application to better understand the teachings of biblical Scriptures.

Clement's successor, Origen (185-254 CE) also taught about Scripture utilizing the metaphor of the human body. Origen argued that as humankind has a body, soul, and spirit, Scripture also has three parts to its meaning. He went on to expand the spiritual meaning of Scripture into a systematic body of teaching. This teaching was created for precise clarification about the nature of the church, including the Christians' relationship to God (Klein, Blomberg and Hubbard 2004, 38-39). Origen's work provided the church a structured method for impacting spiritual transformation through practical teachings of Scripture.

A poignant example of an individual exemplifying spiritual transformation into the identity of Christ comes from the notable martyrdom of Perpetua in 203 CE. Perpetua was a wealthy young mother of an infant boy. Elizabeth Clark describes how Perpetua spoke to her father when he visited her in prison to persuade her to denounce Christianity to avoid the death penalty. Perpetua responded as follows:

> Father . . . 'Do you see this vase lying here . . . or this little pitcher . . . . Now can it be called by any other name than what it is? And he replied, No. Just so, I cannot be said to be anything else than what I am, a Christian. (Clark 1983, 98)

Perpetua depicts a case in point of many early church believers, who were willing to give up their lives, rather than give up their identity in Christ.

Historically, author and theologian Justo Gonzalez, helps us to understand that Christian identity continued to be impacted through the process of teaching, preaching, and the writings of various scholars in the church. Saint Augustine (354-430 CE), Bishop of Hippo, is among the prominent Christian theologians in the church throughout the Middle Ages, continuing even to modern time (Gonzalez 1984, 216). Augustine's initial standard of interpretation of Scripture was written with the intent to lead Christians to love God and to love other people (Klein, Blomberg and Hubbard 2004, 40-41).

Biblical author and scholar, Alister McGrath, describes the eleventh and twelfth centuries as a movement toward a more philosophical approach within Christian writings and instruction. This was an era when a number of critics rose against the Christian faith. In response, many scholars utilized the academic approach of philosophy in defending the Christian faith. At the time, this approach was thought to be needed as a representation of a certain rational explanation of the Christian faith. With this systematic approach in depicting the articles of faith, scholars also thought it would better enrich the outside world's understanding of the Christian faith. Thomas Aquinas and Duns Scotus were among such writers, who used Aristotle's thought processes and writings as a way of merging and systematically displaying the relationship of the several tenets within Christian spirituality (McGrath 1998, 175). Historically the works of scholars and theologians have contributed greatly, in their systematic approach, to enlighten intellectuals in academia and within other secular arenas about the Christian faith.

Experiential Emphasis in Christian Identity

The experiential emphasis of spiritual formation in Christian identity, according to McGrath, emerged in the seventeenth and eighteenth centuries. Historically, the experiential emphasis grew out of anxiety among some church leaders, regarding communication with Christians on the connection of spirituality with realistic daily living. This concern evolved in what became known as "Pietism," meaning "piety" or "godliness" (McGrath 1998, 175). Pietism became a mechanism to formulate a relationship between the relevance of faith and the experiential context of the commonplace believer. Many leaders of the church, most notably in academia, opposed this approach. However, John Wesley (1703-1791) was one who embraced this model of spiritual formation. Wesley advocated that the experience of "living the faith" was warranted in the Christian conversion process (McGrath 1998, 176). Yet, William Warburton, Bishop of Gloucester, was one who argued that Wesley was a "fanatic" who was confusing the common people (Collins 2003, 123). The experiential component of spiritual formation impacts one's Christian identity at a higher level of significance. However, the intellectual is also needed to explain the impact of the experiential.

Nonetheless, McGrath writes, that the historical implication in this experiential dogma within the church impacted the experiential in large numbers of ordinary people to following the way of Jesus. This growth caused Christianity to become relevant with the everyday individual. Whereas the experiential doctrine was in sharp contrast with the intellectuals (resulting in great division within the two groups), it connected faith to one's experience. Spiritual formation now was understood as a heart matter, not just a mind matter (McGrath 1998, 176). This type of spiritual formation resembles that of Christians in the early centuries. Their spiritual formation and Christian identity were together referred to as a connected substance in both, the soul and the spirit of an individual.

Impacting Christian Identity through Community

Consistently throughout history, the church has participated in the formative spiritual process of its members. In accordance with Icenogle, I am reminded that one's individual spiritual transformation is best achieved as a relational group experience within community. Although community experiences within churches have been described by some as a recent contemporary phenomenon; historically, communities of groups have always existed within the church. It is important to interject that humans were created by God as unique beings in relationship within community. It is evident in Scripture that while God is different from humankind, God enjoys community with humankind. Also, the earthly (historical) Jesus lived in community. Therefore, community is a universal cord which connects God with humankind (Icenogle 1994, 10). Community provides human beings relational connections with each other.

Moreover, as I reflect on Icenogle's writings regarding the ongoing relational connections of community, I am aware of how the church has historically identified the need for structured biblical instruction and spiritual disciplines of the Christian faith. These spiritual disciplines have been established historically by the church as vitally necessary for the experiential transformational process of believers in the way of Jesus. Historically, this intentional and consistent movement in the spiritual formation process continues to be relevant to impact Christians' identity within the church. This course of action within Christianity goes beyond the sheer intellectual knowledge about God, but transforms Christians into disciples of Jesus Christ (Icengole 1994).

Utilizing the label of "Christian," as suggested by Judith Lieu, provides a definition of Christianity with both inclusions and exclusions regarding the concept of Christianity. Moreover, this label is not only a description of an identity; but to a greater extent, it brings into existence the being of identity (Lieu 2004, 252). Based on Christian teachings, Christianity is about Jesus Christ bringing wholeness to humankind's essential self for reconciliation back to God. Therefore, our identity in Christ is ordained by God, and can be sustained as a truth.

What is more, this truth is grounded in unyielding biblical and theological foundations that have remained historically congruent for more than twenty centuries. Thus, awareness of our Christian identity is imperative for our spiritual and emotional wholeness. This identity is centered in Jesus Christ, the second person of The Triune God. Furthermore, Jesus reveals in His prayer that the disciples were a gift to Him from God. The Father conveyed in John: "All mine are yours and yours are mine; and I have been glorified in them" (Jn. 17:10). It is interesting that, "Christians often think of Jesus as God's gift to us; we rarely think of ourselves as God's gift to Jesus" (Carson 1980, 184). As stated in John (17:10) and quoted above, according to Gundry, Jesus' disciples belong jointly to Him and God, and they have persisted to acknowledge Jesus as Christ (Gundry 2010, 441). It is noteworthy to point out that we, as humans, may not fully comprehend ourselves as gifts given to Jesus for our redemption and reconciliation back to God; nevertheless, we can read in Scripture that this is a truth.

To better understand their Christian identity, the community of Christians must first have an awareness of their origin as created human beings. St. James Christian Center's members (where I attend) are primarily African-Americans, or often referred as black people. They often identified themselves as a minority race within the United States of America. Many African-American church members (along with many blacks) have experienced an inferiority complex, due to historically enduring racism and classism within the majority cultural. Yet, according to Omar M. McRoberts, sociology professor, the community of the historical black church is a history of diverse associations embedded in a wider scope of political, social and economic contexts. Furthermore, he points out the following:

> Throughout slavery, blacks formed religious congregations
> in secret . . . communities were . . . dictated by the
> whims of the plantations slave system, and faith-based

> development . . .. From these . . . sprang countless African-American social, economic, and political institutions, including schools, insurance companies, banks, and social service organizations. (McRoberts 2001, 1-2)

Therefore, it is imperative that all African-American Christians remember they were, first and foremost, created in the image of God.

In addition, God provided African-Americans from the beginning of time (along with all humankind) core longings as relational blessings of connections with Him. Consequently, an inferiority complex is not truth for anyone to believe about their self. Noted African American historian, Carter Godwin Woodson (1875-1950) is attributed with the following; ". . . If you make a person feel that he or she is inferior, you do not have to compel them to accept an inferior status, for they will seek it themselves . . ." (Woodson, 2015). Therefore, cognitively, African-Americans must sustain an awareness that it was Adam and Eve through their sin of disobedience, who allowed all humankind to be separated from God. Yet, God has created a plan of reconciliation through Jesus to redeem humankind back to Him.

In Romans we read, "But God proves his love for us in that while we still were sinners Christ died for us" (Rom. 5:8 NRSV). Gundry writes that "by contrast, God demonstrates his love for us as sinners rather than as good and righteous people" (Gundry 2010, 586). Therefore, we can understand that even as sinners, God valued us so much that He redeemed us through the death of His Son, Jesus. Significant and highly favored, we are restored by God to be in relationship with Him through the work of Jesus (Shaw 2013, xvii). Knowing our identity in Christ removes internal emotional struggles of confusion and identity crisis. The Apostle Peter points out that we know our purpose is to praise God, to ". . . proclaim the mighty acts of him who called you out of darkness into his marvelous light" (1 Pet. 2:9b NRSV). Gundry describes this verse as God in the following, "exemplifies such a proclamation—not a private thanksgiving, but a public recital of his saving acts" (Gundry 2010, 943). We can also determine from this passage that we, as Christians, are God's special people.

Accordingly, Christians can assess from the biblical writers that humankind naturally is inclined to think, though inappropriately, of their own individual self. However, these writers also illustrate the negative outcomes of such thoughts. Subsequently, they exhort their readers to take on a new mind, and not to consider their ability to make right choices without God's directions. Thereby, we read that these writers assailed natural self-esteem, knowledge, and self-doubt regarding their identity in Christ. The writers encouraged the learner to receive their self-worth and self-esteem only from God, in Christ (Cohen 1988, 134). Therefore, the way to combat low self-esteem, low self-worth and unknown identity is to have a personal identity, esteem, and faith in God through Christ Jesus.

CHAPTER EIGHT:
REFLECTIONS AND CONCLUSION

Brian Williams, the long-time anchor of NBC Nightly News, was caught lying, padding his resume. The media and others are aghast, asking questions like, 'Why did he lie given he had reached the top of his profession and earned millions of dollars per year? (Bedrick, February 11, 2015)

(CNN)—Moreover, Tareq and Michaele Salahi, the Virginia ex-couple who famously—or infamously—crashed President Obama's first White House state dinner. Ralph Napierski, a German self-declared bishop . . . . at the Vatican. The fake bishop played the part of cardinal. (Ravitz (CNN), March 5, 2013)

. . . Sadie Delany had just turned 106 and was on her own for the first time in her life. Always known as one-half of a pair, her identity forged since birth as one of the Delany sisters, Sadie suddenly found herself, unwillingly, an individual. (Delany and Hearth, 1997)

The scenarios above depict how humankind's identity can be distorted if it is not rooted in the identity of Jesus Christ. Identity in Christ secures one's God esteem, which is imperative for avoiding the emotional grip of a distorted and transient self identity that results in its collapse. Nonetheless, many of us, as Christians, have defined our identity, achievement, self-worth and self-image by customary rules put forth by the cultural we live in.

To address the needs for individuals to educate themselves in Christian identity, I created a study to evaluate the effectiveness of a small group experience in impacting Christian identity. As stated earlier, this book is an outgrowth of my doctor of ministry research project. The purpose of the project was to impact the Christian identity among a select group of members from St. James Christian Center, Columbus, Ohio through their participation in a Pathways Curriculum (Thomas and Franks 2009) small group. This project's research results indicated that the small group experience was effective in participants understanding their core longings that impact their Christian identity. Furthermore, the curriculum introduced the participants to a process of spiritual formation, which included discipleship in the context of a small group. Additionally, it also began a transformative emotional healing process for the participants, and an experience of an internal spiritual renewal.

Being that many of the participants were college educated with professional jobs, they initially proudly defined their identity in their profession. As they proceeded in the small group experience, they became more aware of their core longings in connection to their Christian identity. This awareness became poignant in several conversations among participants, to desist associating their identity with their profession. They also became more enlightened of the importance of being in relationship with others through a small group experience.

Participants understanding their perception of God also impact how they view their identity in Christ. Based on *Healing Care Groups*

Curriculum (Wardle 2001), it is important to connect how we view God as our Father with how we have connected this image of God with our earthly father. How we have experienced love with our earthly father, can often be projected onto how we view and relate to our Heavenly Father.

The participants underwent a process through knowledge, experiential, and spiritual disciplines toward impacting their identity in Christ. In that process, they needed, first, to understand about God's unconditional love, including His relational blessings of core longings. The next step in the process, the participants needed to be aware, how after *The Fall*, humankind's consciousness of God was distorted, resulting in them experiencing "core longing deficits." Thirdly, there was need to recognized God's plan of restoration for humankind in Jesus Christ through the power of The Holy Spirit. Fourthly, the participants needed knowledge of how their emotional wounds and dysfunctional behaviors negatively impact their relationships with God, self and others. Lastly, through the formational counseling/healing structure, the participants experienced how to incorporate their core longings, self-fulfilling behaviors, and unprocessed emotional wounds for positively impacting their identity in Christ. Utilizing the *Pathways Curriculum*, demonstrated a structure (which included the Wardle's formational healing prayer model) that was successful in impacting participants' Christian identity within a small group format.

I feel this book has the ability to assert itself in discussions regarding the myth of self-esteem with the truth of God esteem, which impacts one's identity in Christ. Through the formational counseling and prayer model, people can experience the joy of integrating their self-identity with their identity in Christ. The formational counseling concepts are imperative for people to learn the myths of self-esteem and the truth of God-esteem, which so impacts Christian identity.

As stated earlier, many Christians define themselves based on perverse early life messages they have received from other emotionally wounded people. The recipients of such messages experience an internal "personal identity crisis." Consequently, when we are not grounded in knowing our identity in Christ, our belief system is distorted, and these distorted beliefs can contribute to our identity crisis. However, utilizing the principles of formational counseling and formational prayer, individuals will positively be impacted in their Christian identity.

The approach set forth in this book, demonstrates a structure for leading others in an awareness of their past emotional unprocessed wounds. Those unhealed wounds that have negatively impacted their Christian identity. The awakening of pain that has never been addressed allows the person to better move forward on their journey to a life of transformation. Dr. Wardle better addresses this transformation possibility as follows: in the following:

> The Christian life is far more than being freed from the consequences of sin and/or understanding propositional truth related to Christian beliefs. The Christian life is a transforming journey, with clearly defined destination, ongoing challenges that provide opportunities for personal growth . . . .(Wardle 2004, 11)

A process of a transformational change that Dr. Wardle writes about can be addressed through believers embracing the model of formational counseling principles. Since this model provides a structure that is plainly defined, it offers a framework for personal healing, and growth that leads to positively impacting one's identity in Christ. Once a person experience the healing that results from journeying through the process in this model, the person is free from the bondage of false beliefs and distorted thinking regarding their identity. Ultimately, it is the ministry and work of the Holy Spirit.

CONCLUDING THOUGHTS

Imagine a hospital nursery. You stand in the hall and gaze through the window at a room full of newborn babies. They lie in acrylic trays wrapped in pink or blue blankets. They are all important and deserve attention and care. They are equally valuable. The treatment the baby receives depends on the nature of the caregivers, not the worth of the baby. (Ledford 2012, Introduction)

Many of us, even as Christians, are suffering from unprocessed emotional wounds that occurred during our early years. Subsequently, humans who experience such emotional wounds (that are unprocessed) also experience false beliefs of who they are, including their personal worth. As previously stated, my personal journey goals included building upon an awareness that my self-worth is in my Christian identity as a child of God. My self-worth is not rooted in my performance behaviors, which included working to please everyone in my circle of influence. In reflection, I am more aware how for years, I was steeped in the myth of earning self-esteem. I did not have an awareness of embracing the truth of God's esteem.

As I become more cognizant of my core longing deficits, I increase my awareness of the need to seek approval and affirmation from others. In reflection, Howard Thurman writings influenced my understanding of how I have often experienced a core longing deficit of significance. I came to realize that part of my feelings of insignificance was due to my ethnic heritage as an African-American. Thurman writes that most people live at the edge of survival or with their "backs against the wall . . . that they are the poor, the disinherited, and the dispossessed" (Thurman 1976, 13). Furthermore, Thurman constructs a theory on how society's "disinherited" people can better understand who they are in light of the historical Jesus. Thurman constructed a personhood of the historical Jesus within the context of His earthly Jewish community. He includes in his description several factors to consider about Jesus' earthly life in the following:

> Jesus was a poor Jew . . . . Jesus was a member of a minority group in the midst of a larger dominant and controlling group . . . . Jesus was not a Roman citizen . . . . For the privileged and underprivileged alike, if the individual puts at the disposal of the Spirit the needful dedication and disciplines, he can live effectively . . . . (Thurman 1976, 15-108)

Reading Thurman's writings in my doctoral studies, has influenced my ability to amalgamate the foundations of this book within myself. Furthermore, I am on the journey in counteracting my core longing deficits through replacing my false beliefs with the truth rooted in Scripture for example in the following: I am a child of God. I am in relationship with God through Jesus Christ. Also, I am more than a conqueror, because I have been redeemed from the curse of the fall. This book addresses the structures of healing needed for my structural position to encounter Jesus for my emotional healing. Based on this framework on healing, I am experiencing positive movement toward wholeness relating to my emotional upheavals resulting from my core longing deficits.

In this book, I describe how the Apostle Paul characterized his spiritual and transformational experience into his new order of Christian identity. He likens himself to being dead to the old order of things in his life, because of his unification with Christ. I am reminded of the Ohio State University's sports mascot named Brutus, who has been described as fifty-five years old. Yet, at the football games, Brutus is seen with enormous youthful energy jumping, clapping etc, not because of Brutus' ability. However, Brutus has a lot of energy due to the person that is inside Brutus. This metaphor gives me meaning in the Apostle Paul words that, "I am have been crucified with Christ; and it is no longer I who live, but it is Christ who lives in me. And the life I now live in the flesh I live by faith in the Son of God, who loved me and gave himself for me" (Gal. 2:19-20).

The truth that I am a child of God, and created in His image is imperative knowledge for me. Often I have defined myself by self-esteem myths as an isolated individual disconnected from how I am created in God's image. Mark Driscoll, author and pastor, points out the following:

> We see ourselves almost exclusively, in individualistic terms, at the very most, perhaps, part of a family and a role and an identity within the context of a family. The result is, then, we tend to have an identity based upon things . . . All these things may help explain us, but they do not define us. (Driscoll, http://markdriscoll.org/sermons/i-am-in-christ/ accessed October 22, 2015)

God sees me as positioned in Christ who made the ultimate sacrifice so I can experience God's love. According to the first chapter of Ephesians, the Apostle Paul says that I have been adopted into God's family, including the following: I am blessed, faithful, chosen, blameless, holy, forgiven, and reconciled back to God with hope that includes spiritual inheritance.

As I persist in my life's journey, my expectation is to impact Christian identity in others through an emotional healing ministry based on the formational counseling principles discussed in this book. Numerous Christians have unprocessed traumatic emotional wounds, which are the basis of their false beliefs that facilitates distorted views of their self-worth, self-concept, and self-identity. Also, these wounds are the basis for misrepresentation in how they view God that also negatively impacts their identity in Christ.

My Christian identity continues to be impacted when I meditate on those words Dr. Wardle imparted in me during that initial class in my doctorate academic journey, which is also stated in chapter one of this book. He said to me that, "That there is nothing you can do to make God love you anymore and there is nothing you can do to make Him love you any less. You are chosen, you are beloved, and you are empowered". I bring to a close this book with the words of the Apostle Paul in the New Testament. While these words are previously stated in this book, I am always so uplifted each time I read the following passage in Galatians:

> I have been crucified with Christ; and it is no longer I who live, but it is Christ who lives in me. And the life I now live in the flesh I live by faith in the Son of God, who loved me and gave himself for me. (Gal. 2:19-20)

Therefore, Who am I? "I am a chosen race" as recorded in 1 Peter 2:9. While this verse speaks of a race, it is given to me, since individuals are the composition of a race. The chosen race includes all colors, all humans, and all nationalities. Moreover, Who am I? I am chosen and my identity is in Christ. Consequently, I no longer acquiesce to the myth of self-esteem, but I have accepted the truth of my esteem is in God. I have been created in the image of God, and reconciled back to Him through the redemption of Jesus Christ. As a result, my personal expedition is best summed up in the following song lyrics, Changed by the Gospel singer, Tramaine Hawkins:

Changed
A change, a change has come over me.
He changed my life and now I'm free
He washed away all my sins, and he made me whole.
Lord you've changed my life complete . . . .

REFERENCE

Ablow, Keith. 2007. *Living the truth: transform your life through the power of insight and honesty*. New York, NY: Little, Brown and Company.

Allender, Dan B. 1999. *The healing path: how the hurts in your past can lead you to a more abundant life*. Colorado Springs, Colorado: Waterbrook Press.

Anderson, Neil T. 2000. *Victory over the darkness*. Ventura, California: Regal Books Publishers.

Austrian, Sonia G. 2002. *Developmental theories through the life cycle*. New York, NY: Columbia University Press.

Banai, Erez; Mario Mikulincer, and Phillip R. Shaver. 2005. "Self object" needs In kohut's self psychology: links with attachment, self-cohesion, affect Regulation, and adjustment. *Psychoanalytic Psychology* Vol. 22, No. 2: 224-260.

Barnard, Jody. 2009. Unity in Christ: The Purpose of Ephesians. *The Expository Times:* 168.

Bill, Brent J. and Beth A Booram . 2012. *Awaken your senses: exercises for exploring the wonder of God*. Downers Grove, IL: InterVaristy Press.

Blast, Anthony, J., Jean Duhaime, and Paul-Andre Turcotte. 2002. *Handbook of early Christianity: social science approaches*. Walnut Creek, CA: Altamira Press.

Borg, Marcus, J. 2003. *The heart of Christianity: rediscovering a life of faith*. New York, N.Y.: HarperCollins Publishers.

Boyd, Gregory. 2010. *Present perfect: Finding God in the now*. Grand Rapids, Michigan: Zondervan Publishing.

Bridges, Jerry. 2012. *Who am I?: identity in Christ*. info@Cruciform Press. Com: Cruciform Press.

Bromiley, Geoffrey W. and Everett F. Harrison. 1982. *The international standard Bible encyclopedia – Volume: 2*. Grand Rapids, MI: W. B. Eerdmans.

Browning, Don S.; David Polk and Ian S. Evison. 1989. *The education of the practical theologian: responses to Joseph Hough and John Cobb's Christian identity and theological education*. Atlanta, Georgia: Scholars Press.

Bouson, Brooks. 1989. *The empathic reader: a study of the narcissistic character and the drama of the self*. Amherst, MA: University of Massachusetts Press.

Carson, D.A. 1980. *The Farewell discourse and final prayer of Jesus: an Exposition of John 14-17*. Grand Rapids, MI: Baker Book House.

Charry, Ellen T. 1997. *By the renewing of your minds: the pastoral function of Christian doctrine*. New York, NY: Oxford University Press.

Childs, Brevard, S. 1993. *Biblical theology of the old and new testaments: theological reflection on the Christian bible*. Minneapolis, MN.: Fortress Press.

Clinebell, Howard. 1995. *Counseling for spirituality empowered wholeness: A hope-centered approach*. New York, NY: Hayworth Pastoral Press.

Cohen, Edmund. 1988. *The Mind of the Bible-Believer*. Amherst, NY: Prometheus Books.

Collins, Kenneth J. 2003. *John Wesley: a theological journey*. Nashville, Tennessee: Abingdon Press.

Cozolino, Louis. 2010. *The neuroscience of psychotherapy: healing the social Brain*. New York, NY: W. W. Norton and Company.

Crabb, Larry. 1997. *Connecting: Healing for ourselves and our relationships*. Nashville, Tennessee: W Publishing Group.

Curtis, Brent and John Eldredge. 1997. *The sacred romance: Drawing closer to the heart of God*. Nashville, TN: Thomas Nelson Inc.

Dawes, Milton. 2010. Developing a self: A general semantics way. *ETC: A Review of General Semantics* Vol: 67, Issue: 1 (January): 79.

de Caussade, Jean-Pierre. 1989. *The sacrament of the present moment*. San Francisco, CA: Harper Publishing.

Delany, Sarah L. and Amy Hill Hearth. 1997. *On my own at 107*. New York, NY: Harper Collins Publishers Inc.

Douglas, J.D. and Merrill C. Tenney. 1987. *New international Bible dictionary*. Grand Rapids, Michigan: Zondervan Publishing.

Durken, Daniel. 2009. *New collegeville Bible commentary: New Testament*. Collegeville , Minnesota: Liturgical Press.

Dunn, James D.G. and John W. Rogerson. 2003. *Eerdmans commentary on the bible*. Grand Rapids, MI.: W.B. Eerdmans Publisher.

Ehrman, Bart D. 2008. *God's problem: how the Bible fails to answer our most important question---why we suffer*. New York, NY: Harper Collins Publishers.

Ellens, Harold J. and Wayne G. Rollins. 2004. *Psychology and the Bible: a new way to read the Scriptures*. Westport, CT: Praeger Publishers.

Ellis, Albert. 2005. *The myth of self-esteem: how rational emotive behavior therapy can change your life forever*. Amherst, NY: Prometheus Books.

Erickson, Millard J. 1995. *God in three persons*. Grand Rapids, Michigan: Baker Books. _____. 1992. *Introducing Christian doctrine*. Grand Rapids, Michigan: Baker Books.

Fenlon, Francois. 1992. *The seeking heart*. Jacksonville, FL: Seed Sowers Publishing.

Frend, W.H.C. 1984. *The rise of Christianity*. Philadelphia, PA.: Fortress Press.

Garrett, James Leo, Jr. 2007. *Systematic theology*. North Richland Hills, Texas: Bibal Press.

Geiger, Eric. 2008. *Identity: Who You Are In Christ*. Nashville, TN: B&H Publishing Group.

Gilby, Thomas. 1951. *St. Thomas Aquinas: philosophical texts*. London, England: Oxford University Press.

Gombis, Timothy G. 2010. *The drama of ephesians: participating in the triumph of God*. Downers Grove, IL: Intervarsity Press.

Gonzalez, Justo L. 1984. *The story of Christianity: the early church to the dawn of the reformation*. New York, N.Y: Harper Collins Publishers.

Gorman, Michael J. 2004. *Apostle of the crucified Lord: a theological introduction to paul and his letters*. Grand Rapids, MI: William B. Eerdmans Publishing Co.

Green, Arthur. 1996. To live as God's image. *Tikkun* 11, Issue 1 (January): 66-72.

Green, Michael. 2004. *Evangelism in the early church*. Grand Rapids, MI.: W.B. Eerdmans Publisher.

Green, Viviane. 2003. *Emotional development in psychoanalysis, attachment theory, and neuroscience: creating connections*. Hove, England: Brunner-Routledge, Publisher.

Grenz, Stanley J. 2004. Jesus as the Imago Dei: Image–of-God Christology And the non-linear linearity of theology. *Journal of the Evangelical Theological Society* 47, No. 4 (December): 3-7.

_____. 1994. *Theology for the community of God*. Grand Rapids, Michigan: William B. Eerdmans Publishing Co.

Grudem, Wayne. 1994. *Systematic theology: an introduction to biblical doctrine*. Grand Rapids, Michigan: Zondervan Publishing House.

Gundry, Robert H. 2010. *Commentary on the New Testament: verse-by-verse explanations with a literal translation*. Peabody, Massachusetts: Hendrickson Publishers Marketing, LLC.

Hahn, Scott and Curtis Mitch. 2010. *The Ignatius Catholic Study Bible New Testament*. San Francisco, CA: Ignatius Press.

Halley, Anne Medaglia. 2009. *Developmental formational prayer workbook*. Ashland, OH: Ashland Theological Seminary.

Harrison, Nonna Verna. 2010. *God's many-splendored image: theological Anthropology for Christian formation*. Grand Rapids, MI: Baker Academic.

Helm, Paul. 2004. *John Calvin's ideas*. Oxford, England: Oxford University Press.

Heschel, Abraham J. 1962. *The prophets*. New York, NY.: Harper Collins Publishers Inc..

Hill, Jonathan. 2011. *Christianity: how a despised sect from a minority religion came to dominate the roman empire*. Minneapolis, MN: Fortress Press.

Hill, Napoeleon. 2003. *Think and grow rich: the landmark best seller now revised and updated for the 21st century*. New York, NY.: The Penguin Group Publishers.

Hodgson, Peter C. and Robert H. King. 1994. *Christian theology: an introduction to its traditions and tasks*. Minneapolis, MN.: Fortress Press.

Hoekem, Anthony A. 1989. *Saved by grace*. Grand Rapids, MI: William B. Eerdmans Publishing Co.

Hoehner, Harold W. 2002. *Ephesians: an exegetical commentary*. Grand Rapids, MI: Baker Academic.

Hoffman, Marie T. 2011. *Toward mutual recognition*: relational psychoanalysis *and the Christian narrative*. New York, NY: Taylor and Francis Group.

Holmes, Christopher R. J. 2013. The person and work of Christ revisited: in Conversation with Karl Barth. *Anglican Theological Review* (Winter).

Holmgren, Fredrick C. 1999. *The Old Testament: the Significance of Jesus.* Grand Rapids, MI: Wm. B. Eerdmans Publishing Co.

Honess, Terry and Krysia Yardley. 1987. *Self and identity: perspectives across the lifespan.* London, England: Routledge and Kegan Paul Publisher.

Horton, Michael. 2011. *The Christian faith.* Grand Rapids, Michigan: Zondervan.

Icenogle, Weldon Gareth. 1994. *Biblical foundations for small group ministry.* Downers Grove, IL: Inter Varsity Press.

Jewett, Paul K. 1991. *God, creation and revelation: a neo-evangelical theology.* Grand Rapids, Michigan: Wm. B. Eerdmans Publishing Co.

Johnson, Patrick, Walter Buboltz and Eric Seemann. 2003. Ego Identity Status: A Step in the Differentiation Process. *Journal of Counseling and Development* 81, Issue 2 (Spring): 191-195.

Jones, L, Gregory. 1995. Embodying forgiveness: a theological analysis. Grand Rapids, Michigan: William B. Eerdmans Publishing Co.

Kirwan, William T. 1984. *Biblical concepts for Christian counseling: A case for integrating psychology and theology.* Grand Rapids, MI: Baker Academic.

Klein, William W.; Craig L. Blomberg and Robert L. Hubbard, Jr. 2004. *Introduction to biblical interpretation.* Nashville, Tennessee: Thomas Nelson, Inc.

Ledford, Terry L. 2012. *Parables for a wounded heart: overcoming the wounds to your self-esteem and transforming your perception of you.* Middletown, DE. Serenitime Media.

Leick, Nini and Marianne Davidsen-Nielsen. 1991. *Healing pain: attachment, loss, and grief therapy.* New York, NY: Routledge Publisher.

Lewis, C. S. 1997. *The joyful Christian*. New York, New York: Simon and Schuster.

Lieu, Judith M. 2004. *Christian identity in the jewish and graeco-roman world*. Oxford, England: Oxford University Press.

Lloyd-Jones, D. M. 1979. *The unsearchable riches of Christ: an exposition of Ephesians 3:1 to 21*. Grand Rapids, MI: Baker Book House.

Logan, Julie. 2015. *Theories of counseling-self psychology.html,* accessed January 24, 2015.

Louth, Andrew. 2001. *Ancient Christian commentary on Scripture: Old Testament I Genesis 1-11*. Downers Grove, IL: InterVarsity Press.

MacArthur, John. 2005. *The macarthur Bible commentary*. Nashville, Tennessee: Thomas Nelson, Inc.

May, Gerald G. 1992. *Care of mind/care of spirit: a psychiatrist explores spiritual direction*. San Francisco, CA: Harper Collins Publishing.

McDermott, Gerald R. 2010. *The great theologians: a brief guide*. Downers Grove, Illinois: IVP Academic Publishers.

McFarland, Ian A. 2009. *Creation and humanity*. Louisville, Kentucky: Westminster John Knox Press.

McGee, Robert S. 2003. *The search for significance*. Nashville, TN: Thomas Nelson.

McGrath, Alister E. 1998. *Historical theology: an introduction to the history of christian thought*. Malden, MA: Blackwell Publishing.

McRay, John. 2003. *Paul: his life and teaching*. Grand Rapids, MI: Baker Academic.

Mintle, Linda S. 2002. *Breaking free from a negative self-image: finding God's true reflection when your mirror lies.* Lake Mary, Florida: Charisma House Publisher.

Moltmann, Jurgen. 1993. *God in creation: A new theology of creation and the Spirit of God.* Minneapolis, MN.: Fortress Press.

Mursell, Mursell. 2001. *The story of Christian Spirituality: two thousand years, from east to west.* Oxford, England: Lion Publishing.

Neese, Zach. 2012. *How to worship a king.* www.gatewaycreate.com.

Niebuhr, Reinhold. 1964. *The nature and destiny of man: a Christian interpretation volume II: human destiny.* Louisville, Kentucky: Westminster John Knox Press.

Nouwen, Henri J. 1972. *The wounded healer: ministry in contemporary society.* New York, NY: Bantam Doubleday Dell Publishing Group.

Oden, Thomas C. 2006. *Systematic theology: volume three life in the Spirit.* Peabody, Massachusetts: Henrickson Publishers, Inc.

Payne, Leanne. 1995. *The healing presence: Curing the soul through union with Christ.* Grand Rapids, MI: Baker Books.

Plummer, Deborah. 2005. *Helping adolescents and adults to build self-esteem.* London, England: Publisher: Jessica Kingsley.

Radmacher, Earl D.; Ronald B. Allen; H. Wayne House. 1999. *Nelson's new illustrated bible commentary.* Nashville, Tennessee: Thomas Nelson Inc.

Reiss, Moshe. 2011. Adam: created in the image and likeness of God. *Jewish Bible Quarterly* 39, Issue 3 (July-September): 181.

Rivera, Miguela. 2014. On developing self-identity. *The Hispanic Outlook in Higher Education* Vol: 34, Issue 14 (April 21): 30.

Saunders, Stanley P. 2002. "Learning Christ": Eschatology and spiritual Formation in new testament Christianity. *Interpretation Journal* 56, Issue 2 (April): 155-177.

Schaff, Philip. 2006. *History of the Christian Church: Volume 1*. Peabody, Massachusetts: Hendrickson Publishers, Inc.

Scheele, Paul-Werner. 1998. Our common calling. *The Ecumenical Review* (July): 351.

Schore, Allan N. 2002. The neurobiology of attachment and early personality organization. *Journal of Prenatal & Perinatal Psychology & Health* Vol: 16, Issue: 3 (Spring): 249.

_____. 1994. *Affect regulation and the origin of the self: the neurobiology of emotional development*. Hillsdale, NJ: Lawrence Erlbaum Associates Publisher.

Schwartz, Jeffrey M. and Rebecca Gladding. 2011. *You are not your brain: the 4-step solution for changing bad habits, ending unhealthy thinking, and taking control of your life*. New York, NY: The Penguin Group.

Seamands, David A. 1981. *Healing for damaged emotions*. Colorado Springs, Colorado: David C. Cook, Publisher.

Seamands, Stephens. 2005. *Ministry in the image of God: The Trinitarian shape of Christian service*. Downers Grove, IL: Inter Varsity Press Books.

_____. 2003. *Wounds that heal: Bringing our hurts to the cross*. Downers Grove, IL: Inter Varsity Press Books.

Shaw, Robert B., Jr. 2013. *Created for significance: discovering our human core longings, who defines us, and how we reverse identity theft.* Bloomington, IN: WestBow Press.

Sheets, Dutch. 2007. *Becoming who you are: embracing the power of your identity in Christ.* Bloomington, Minnesota: Bethany House Publishers.

Sibley, Towner W. 2005. Clones of God: Genesis 1:26-28 and the image of God in the hebrew Bible. *Interpretation Journal* (October): 341.

Siegel, Daniel J. and Mary Hartzell. 2003. *Parenting from the inside out: how a deeper self-understanding can help you raise children who thrive.* New York, NY: Penguin Group.

Stott, John R. W. 1958. *Basic Christianity.* Downers Grove, Illinois: IVP Books.

Thomas, Donna. 2007. *The healing Christ in community.* Ashland, OH: Rose Publishers.

Thomas, Donna and Frank Jeffs. 2009. *Pathways next steps small group ministry.* Wooster, OH. Jeff.franks@woosternewhope.org.

Thurman, Howard. 1976. *Jesus and the disinherited.* Boston, MA: Beacon Press.

Trimm, Cindy. 2011. *The 40 Day Soul Fast: Your Journey to Authentic Living.* Shippensburg, PA.: Destiny Image Publishers, Inc.

Van Der Kool, Cornelis and Donald Mader. 2005. *As in a mirror: John Calvin and Karl Barth on knowing God: a diptych.* Boston, MA.: Brill Publisher.

Volf, Miroslav. 1998. *After our likeness: the Church as the image of the Trinity.* Grand Rapids, MI: William B. Eerdmans Publisher.

Waltke, Bruce K. 2001. *Genesis a commentary.* Grand Rapids, Michigan: Zondervan Publishers.

Wardle, Terry. 2007. *Strong winds and crashing waves: meeting Jesus in the memories of traumatic events.* Abilene, TX: Leafwood Publishers.

_____. 2004. *Helping others on the journey: a guide for those who seek to mentor others to maturity in Christ.* Kent, England: Sovereign World.

_____. 2004. *Outrageous love transforming power.* Abilene, TX: Leafwood Publishers.

_____. 2001. *Healing care groups: leader's guide.* Ashland, Ohio: Ashland Theological Seminary.

_____. 2001. *Healing care healing prayer.* Abilene, TX: Leafwood Publishers.

_____. 1998. *Draw close to the fire.* Abilene, TX: Leafwood Publishers.

Westermann, Claus. 1994. *Genesis 1—11: a continental commentary.* Minneapolis, MN: First Fortress Press.

Willard, Dallas. 2010. *A place for truth: leading thinkers explore life's hardest questions.* Downers Grove, Illinois: IVP Books.

Wright, N. T. 2006. *Simply Christian.* New York, NY: Harper Collins Publishers.

_____. 1993. *The climax of the covenant: Christ and the law in pauline theology.* Minneapolis, MN: Fortress Press.